most loved cookbooks compilation index

Most Loved Appetizers

Most Loved Brunches

Most Loved Casseroles

Most Loved Cookies

Most Loved Festive Baking

Most Loved Holiday Favourites

Most Loved Main Courses

Most Loved Salads & Dressings

Most Loved Slow Cooker Creations

Most Loved Stir-fries

Most Loved Summertime Desserts

Most Loved Treats

You'll be delighted with the delicious recipes and helpful tips you'll find in the Most Loved Cookbooks series. To make recipe finding easier, we've created an index of the recipes and tips found in this series of books. Whether you are browsing for a recipe that uses a certain ingredient or you are looking for a specific recipe, this composite index to all 12 books in the series will help you find any recipe from any of the books in one convenient location. Place this index in the book rack with your Most Loved Cookbooks for easy reference.

MOST LOVED COOKBOOKS KEY: Appetizers **AP** • Brunches **BR** • Casseroles **CA** • Cookies **CO** • Festive Baking **FB** • Holiday Favourites **HF** • Main Courses **MC** • Salads & Dressings **SA** • Slow Cooker Creations **SC** • Stir-fries **SF** • Summertime Desserts **SD** • Treats **TR**

recipe index

A Round Of Draft ....10 MC
Acapulco Beef Filet ....25 MC
After-Dinner Mints .... 122 TR
Almond And Raspberry
    Cheesecake........................72 SD
Almond Balls ....110 HF
Almond Balls ....76 CO
Almond Bark, Cranberry............ 103 TR
Almond Biscotti, Cranberry ....49 FB
Almond Butter Cookies, Cherry....26 CO
Almond Buttercream Icing ....16 FB
Almond Chicken ....58 SF
Almond Cranberry Buns,
    Freezer ....110 FB
Almond Filling ....50 CO
Almond Filling ....68 FB
Almond Finger Cookies ....119 CO
Almond Fruit Bark ....107 HF
Almond Glaze ....100 FB
Almond Icing ....102 HF
Almond Liqueur, Strawberries In ..25 SD
Almond Pepper Bread, Crisp ....34 HF
Almond Ring, Fruity ....18 BR
Almond Salad, Orange.................39 SA
Almond Tart, Plum And ....68 FB
Almond Waffles ....32 BR
Angel Food, Burnt Sugar..............38 SD
Angel Roll....................................54 SD
Angel Roll, Tri-Colour ....92 SD
Angel, Lemon Coconut ....39 SD
Aniseed Chicken........................108 MC
Antipasto.....................................27 HF
Antipasto.....................................46 AP
Antipasto Pasta Salad ....90 BR
Appetizers
    Antipasto.................................27 HF
    Best Cheese Ball ....28 HF

Blue Stuffed Mushrooms ....35 HF
Candied Nuts ....24 HF
Crab Tarts.................................36 HF
Crabapple Meatballs ....37 HF
Cranberry Cheese.....................28 HF
Crisp Almond Pepper Bread .....34 HF
Festive Best Cheese Ball...........28 HF
Glazed Meatballs......................37 HF
Good Ol' Nuts 'N' Bolts ....26 HF
Green Onion Whirls.................34 HF
Holiday Whirls ....34 HF
King Artichoke Dip ....30 HF
Seafood Curry Dip...................30 HF
Shrimp Cocktail ....38 HF
Simple Stuffed Mushrooms .....35 HF
Stilton Puffs ....32 HF
Apple
    Baked ....70 TR
    Brown Betty ....71 TR
Apple And Shrimp Salad ....44 SA
Apple Cider Vinaigrette ....110 SA
Apple Cream Quesadillas ....22 SD
Apple Crisp, Caramel ....28 FB
Apple Croissant Pudding..............83 FB
Apple Loaf ....118 TR
Apple Pie, Mum's ....67 FB
Apple Raisin Pancakes ....28 BR
Apple Spice Dressing...................38 SA
Apple Streusel Muffins...............120 TR
Apple Stuffing..............................84 MC
Apple Warmer, Cranberry ....6 SC
Apples In A Phyllo Crust..............76 FB
Applesauce..................................42 SC
Applesauce..................................59 HF
Apricot Balls ....92 CO
Apricot Brandy Truffles ....104 TR
Apricot Dressing..........................78 SA

Apricot Filling..............................89 TR
Apricot Glaze...............................62 TR
Apricot Pork Loin Roast ....58 HF
Apricot Salad ....70 SA
Apricot Sauce .... 122 AP
Apricot Sauce ....70 SA
Apricot Stuffing, Sage And...........76 BR
Apricot Zings...............................89 TR
Arroz Con Pollo ....40 CA
Artichoke Dip ....28 AP
Artichoke Dip, King.....................30 HF
Artichokes, Shrimp And...............68 SF
Asian Citrus Chicken ....56 SF
Asian Dinner, Saucy ....96 SF
Asian Dressing.............................52 SA
Asparagus Chicken, Uptown ....66 BR
Asparagus Omelette....................54 BR
Asparagus Stir-Fry, Shrimp And....70 SF
Autumn Bake ....34 CA
Avocado Salad, Cucumber...........16 SA

Baby Cheddar Tarts.....................97 AP
Baby Swiss Tarts ....97 AP
Bacon
    Jiffy Mushroom Rolls...............98 AP
    Scallops With...........................63 AP
    Spinach Dip #1 ....26 AP
    Wiener Bites ....75 AP
Bacon And Pea Salad ....48 SA
Bacon Dressing, Warm.................34 SA
Bacon Lettuce Salad, Warm ....34 SA
Bacon Omelette, Spinach And .....56 BR
Bacon Varenyky...........................82 HF
Baked Alaska.............................106 SD
Baked Apples...............................70 TR
Baked Ham..................................75 BR
Baked Ham..................................78 MC

MOST LOVED COOKBOOKS KEY: Appetizers **AP** • Brunches **BR** • Casseroles **CA** • Cookies **CO** • Festive Baking **FB** • Holiday Favourites **HF**
Main Courses **MC** • Salads & Dressings **SA** • Slow Cooker Creations **SC** • Stir-fries **SF** • Summertime Desserts **SD** • Treats **TR**

B

Baked Salmon .... 70 BR
Baked Vanilla French Toast .... 36 BR
Bali Sauce .... 76 AP
Bali Wings .... 76 AP
Balls
    Almond .... 76 CO
    Apricot .... 92 CO
    Buried Cherry .... 76 CO
    Cream Cheese .... 92 CO
    Glazed Coffee .... 88 CO
    Peanut Butter Chip .... 90 CO
    Peanut Butter .... 94 CO
    Pecan .... 76 CO
Balsamic Chicken, Spicy .... 46 SF
Balsamic Dressing .... 42 SA
Balsamic Dressing .... 84 BR
Banana Bread .... 20 BR
Banana Bread
    Chocolate .... 94 FB
    Chocolate-Kissed .... 20 BR
    Granola .... 20 BR
Banana Cream Pie .... 63 SD
Banana Frozen Yogurt,
    Strawberry .... 116 SD
Banana Macadamia Sundaes ..... 66 TR
Banana Quesadillas .... 22 SD
Banana Rockets, Frozen .... 106 SD
Banana Split .... 110 SD
Banana Splits, Melon .... 28 SD
Banana Waffles .... 32 BR
Barbecue Beef Ribs .... 46 SC
Barbecue Sauce .... 40 MC
Barbecue Shredded
    Pork Sandwiches .... 108 SC
Barbecue, see Grilling
Barbecued Beef Ribs .... 40 MC
Barbecued Flavoured
    Pork Chops .... 70 MC
Barbecued Flavoured Ribs .... 70 MC
Barbecued Ribs .... 74 MC

Bark, Almond Fruit .... 107 HF
Barley And Rice Pilaf .... 71 HF
Barley Risotto, Herbed .... 32 SC
Bars & Cookies
    Almond Balls .... 110 HF
    Buried Cherry Balls .... 111 HF
    Caramel Slice .... 103 HF
    Chocolate Cherry
        Nanaimo Bars .... 100 HF
    Gingerbread Cookies .... 116 HF
    Lemon Shortbread Slices ... 114 HF
    Marzipan Bars .... 102 HF
    Orange Chocolate Squares . 104 HF
    Orange Cookies .... 109 HF
    Pecan Balls .... 110 HF
    Peppermint Nanaimo Bars .. 100 HF
    Snowballs .... 115 HF
Bars, Orange Date .... 116 BR
Bars, see Squares, Bars & Brownies
Basic Cookie Glaze .... 38 FB
Basic Crepes .... 26 BR
Basic Sugar Cookies .... 38 FB
Basil Dressing .... 43 SA
Basil Dressing, Chili .... 65 SA
Basil Mustard Dressing .... 61 SA
Basil Pesto Croutons .... 120 SA
Basil Pesto, Parsley .... 92 CA
Basil Pie, Tomato .... 44 BR
Baskets, Noodle .... 24 SF
Batter-Ready Ginger Muffins .... 8 HF
Bean And Cashew Salad .... 56 SA
Bean And Turkey Bake .... 65 CA
Bean Casserole, Mediterranean
    Chicken And .... 44 CA
Bean Pot, Sweet .... 40 SC
Bean Salad .... 58 SA
Bean Soup, Turkey Mixed .... 42 HF
Bean Sprout Salad .... 66 SA
Bean Sprouts
    Beef Sprout Rolls .... 68 AP

Spring Rolls .... 88 AP
Bean Sprouts And Peppers .... 120 SF
Bean Stir-Fry, Green .... 106 SF
Beans
    Black Bean Dip .... 8 AP
    Chili Black .... 105 SC
    Confetti .... 78 HF
    Devil's Dip .... 12 AP
    Double Devil's Dip .... 12 AP
    Fruity Salsa .... 36 AP
    Kidney Bean Dip .... 8 AP
    Mexican Snackies .... 54 AP
    Polynesian Meatballs .... 122 AP
    Refried Bean Dip .... 52 AP
    Spreading Forest Fire .... 38 AP
    Turkey Pot, Full-Of- .... 94 SC
    Wieners And .... 106 CA
Beans And Rice, Spicy .... 102 SC
Beans And Sausage, Fruity .... 40 SC
Bean-Stuffed Peppers, Corn And .. 92 SC
Beef
    A Round of Draft .... 10 MC
    Acapulco Beef Filet .... 25 MC
    Autumn Bake .... 34 CA
    Barbecue Beef Ribs .... 46 SC
    Barbecued Beef Ribs .... 40 MC
    Beef And Biscuits .... 48 SC
    Beef And Greens Stir-Fry .... 22 SF
    Beef And Zucchini .... 8 SF
    Beef Bourguignon .... 30 SF
    Beef Creole .... 116 CA
    Beef Curry Hotpot .... 54 SC
    Beef In Black Bean Sauce .... 17 SF
    Beef In Red Wine .... 58 SC
    Beef Vegetable Soup .... 14 SC
    Beef, Cheesy Meat Canapés .. 58 AP
    Beefy Bun Topping .... 66 SC
    Beefy Pepper Dim Sum ..... 104 AP
    Beefy Roll-Ups .... 102 AP
    Bibimbap .... 12 SF

MOST LOVED COOKBOOKS KEY: Appetizers **AP** • Brunches **BR** • Casseroles **CA** • Cookies **CO** • Festive Baking **FB** • Holiday Favourites **HF**
Main Courses **MC** • Salads & Dressings **SA** • Slow Cooker Creations **SC** • Stir-fries **SF** • Summertime Desserts **SD** • Treats **TR**

B

Recipe	Page	Key
Biscuit-Topped Casserole	22	CA
Bolognese Sauce	69	SC
Broiled Herbed Rouladen	24	MC
Bulgogi	38	MC
Buttered Steak And Shrimp	22	MC
Chap Jae	34	SF
Chili	66	SC
Chinese Pepper Steak	52	SC
Chinese-Style Hash	16	CA
Comfort Roast	60	HF
Company Meatloaf	43	MC
Corned Beef Dinner	50	SC
Corned Beef Hash	64	BR
Corned Beef Mousse	30	AP
Crabapple Meatballs	37	HF
Cranberry Meatballs	100	AP
Creamy Greek Bake	10	CA
Creamy Zucchini Wedges	48	BR
Dijon Beef Stew	49	SC
Dilly Beef Dinner	53	SC
Easy Shepherd's Pie	25	CA
Favourite Mushrooms	114	AP
Fiesta Strata	39	BR
French Tourtière	63	HF
Fruity Beef Curry	10	SF
Ginger Beef	16	SF
Ginger Beef Stew	56	SC
Glazed Meatballs	37	HF
Hamburger Pacific	8	CA
Herbed Beef Tenderloin	8	MC
Honey Garlic Meatballs	46	MC
Hot Tamale Two-Step	28	CA
Hungarian Goulash	55	SC
Indian-Spiced Beef	23	SF
Jambalaya Casserole	18	CA
Lasagna	14	CA
Lasagna	68	SC
Lazy Cabbage Roll Casserole	19	CA
Mandarin Beef	37	SF
Maple-Glazed Meatballs	72	AP
Meatball Stew	70	SC
Mexican Enchiladas	64	BR
Mexican Snackies	54	AP
Mushroom-Stuffed Meatloaf	44	MC
No-Fuss Stroganoff	49	MC
One-Dish Meal	12	CA
Onion Beef Ragout	59	SC
Orange Beef And Broccoli	24	SF
Oven Beef Roast	12	MC
Oven Stew	32	CA
Peppercorn Roast	6	MC
Phyllo Lasagna	62	BR
Picadillo Pie	26	CA
Pineapple Beef Stir-Fry	20	SF
Polynesian Meatballs	122	AP
Polynesian Satay	94	AP
Porcupine Meatball Stew	20	CA
Pot Roast	46	SC
Pot Roast Gravy	46	SC
Refried Bean Dip	52	AP
Reuben Bake	38	CA
Salsa-Stuffed Steak	28	MC
Saucy Ginger Beef	14	SF
Sauerkraut Beef Dinner	63	SC
Sesame Kabobs With Spinach	39	MC
Shipwreck	29	CA
Short Ribs	42	MC
Slow Cooker Beef Roast	12	MC
Slow Cooker Fajitas	64	SC
Slow Stroganoff Stew	62	SC
Spanish Meatballs	74	AP
Spicy Beef And Broccoli	26	SF
Spicy Stuffed	14	MC
Squash Stew	32	CA
Steak Bake	60	SC
Steak With Mushrooms And Onions	30	MC
Steak With Spice Coating	20	MC
Stuffed Roast With Red Wine Sauce	15	MC
Sukiyaki Rice Bowl	28	SF
"Sweetish" Meatballs	70	SC
Swiss Steak Casserole	30	CA
Swiss Stew	33	MC
Szechuan Beef	36	SF
Tater-Topped Beef Bake	24	CA
Teener's Dish	11	CA
Tender Beef And Cashews	6	SF
Tex-Mex Taco Soup	22	SC
Thai Noodles	18	SF
Three Pepper Stir-Fry	32	SF
Tortilla Roll-Ups	70	AP
Tournados	28	MC
Tourtière Québécoise	48	MC
Veal Cutlets In Wine Sauce	50	MC
Veal Oscar	16	MC
West Indies Beef	36	CA
Zesty Beef Casserole	6	CA
Zesty Broiled Steak	24	MC
Beef And Biscuits	48	SC
Beef And Greens Stir-Fry	22	SF
Beef And Yam Stew	34	MC
Beef And Zucchini	8	SF
Beef Bourguignon	30	SF
Beef Bourguignon	32	MC
Beef Creole	116	CA
Beef Curry Hotpot	54	SC
Beef In Black Bean Sauce	17	SF
Beef In Pastry	18	MC
Beef In Red Wine	58	SC
Beef Kabobs With Oregano And Onion	36	MC
Beef Oscar	16	MC
Beef Sprout Rolls	68	AP
Beef Vegetable Soup	14	SC
Beefy Bun Topping	66	SC
Beefy Onion Gravy	12	MC
Beefy Pepper Dim Sum	104	AP
Beefy Roll-Ups	102	AP
Beer Marinade	10	MC

MOST LOVED COOKBOOKS KEY: Appetizers **AP** • Brunches **BR** • Casseroles **CA** • Cookies **CO** • Festive Baking **FB** • Holiday Favourites **HF** • Main Courses **MC** • Salads & Dressings **SA** • Slow Cooker Creations **SC** • Stir-fries **SF** • Summertime Desserts **SD** • Treats **TR**

B

Beet Salad ....66 SA	Sparkling Raspberry Punch........6 BR	Blue Stuffed Mushrooms.............35 HF
Beets, Orange-Sauced ....78 HF	Special Spiced Coffee ....10 BR	Blueberries Romanoff ....29 SD
Berries, Juicy ....10 TR	Bibimbap........................12 SF	Blueberry Coffee Cake................ 109 BR
Berries, Swirl Ice Cream With	Biscotti	Blueberry Cream Pancakes ....30 BR
Grilled Cake And ....48 SD	Choco-Cran.........................66 CO	Blueberry Lemon Trifle .... 122 BR
Berry Creamy Waffles ....31 BR	Chocolate-Dipped Nutty ....67 CO	Blueberry Pie ....9 SD
Berry Mini-Cheesecakes............. 104 BR	Cranberry Almond..................49 FB	Blueberry Streusel French Toast ...14 HF
Berry Rhubarb Dumpling	Mandarin Chocolate.................48 FB	Blueberry Topping ....34 BR
Dessert ....16 SD	Nutty ....67 CO	Bocconne Dolce ....52 TR
Best Cheese Ball ....28 HF	Biscuit Fruit Roll.........................12 HF	Boiled Chocolate Cookies............94 CO
Best Drop Cookies........................6 CO	Biscuit Mix	Boiled Raisin Cake ....20 FB
Best Hash Browns.......................17 HF	Mexican Snackies ....54 AP	Bolognese Sauce ....69 SC
Best Pork Chops..........................70 MC	Zucchini Treats .... 101 AP	Bourbon Cookies......................52 CO
Best Rice Salad .... 100 SA	Biscuits ....48 SC	Bourbon Filling......................52 CO
Best Vegetable Dip.....................14 AP	Biscuits, Beef And ....48 SC	Bourguignon, Beef ....30 SF
Betty	Biscuit-Topped Casserole.............22 CA	Bourguignon, Beef ....32 MC
Brown.............................71 TR	Bites, Sacher Torte ....78 CO	Bowl, Lemon Grass Pork........... 102 SF
Fresh Fruit ....71 TR	Black Bean Dip ....8 AP	Bowl, Sukiyaki Rice ....28 SF
Rhubarb ....71 TR	Black Bean Sauce........................52 SF	Bowls, Orange Blossom............. 122 SD
Bev's Chicken Casserole .... 114 MC	Black Bean Sauce, Beef In ....17 SF	Bowls, Tortilla......................32 SA
Beverages	Black Bean Sauce, Seafood In.......84 SF	Braised Vegetables .... 116 SF
Brandy Wassail ....20 HF	Black Bean Shrimp Noodles ....82 SF	Bran Cereal Cookies ....24 CO
Café Latté............................10 BR	Black Bean Stir-Fry,	Bran Topping, Walnut.................10 SD
Caramel Hot Chocolate ....6 SC	Chicken And......................52 SF	Brandied Peaches ....70 TR
Champagne Orange Juice ....6 BR	Black Beans, Chili .... 105 SC	Brandy Sauce, Cinnamon.................14 TR
Christmas Punch ....20 HF	Black Forest Cookies..................78 CO	Brandy Truffles, Apricot .... 104 TR
Christmas Spirit ....23 HF	Black Forest Decadence...............14 FB	Brandy Wassail ....20 HF
Cranberry Apple Warmer ....6 SC	Black Moons, Halloween .... 122 CO	Bread Bowl ....26 AP
Cranberry Mulled Wine ....10 SC	Blackened Chicken ....30 SA	Bread Crumbs, Homemade.............80 CA
Fresh Herb Tea ....9 BR	Blackened Chicken	Bread Pudding ....82 FB
Hot Buttered Cranberry.............10 SC	Caesar Salad...........................30 SA	Bread Pudding, Raisin ....86 HF
Hot Spiced Cranberry.............10 SC	Blackened Snapper.....................62 MC	Bread Stuffing ....84 MC
Hot Tea Wassail ....8 SC	Bliss Bars......................53 FB	Bread Stuffing, Raisin 'N'............14 MC
Irish Cream.........................22 HF	Blisters..................38 AP	Bread Stuffing, Spicy
Mango Smoothies...................8 BR	Blondie Brownies...................60 FB	Sausage And........................44 SC
Mulled Wine ....10 SC	Blossoms, Peanut ....56 CO	Breads
Mulled Wine ....22 HF	Blue Cheese Dressing .... 107 SA	Blisters......................38 AP
Party Eggnog.........................24 HF	Blue Cheese Tarts, Date And..... 106 AP	Cheese Thins ....39 AP
Pineapple Citrus Punch ....8 BR	Blue Cheesecake......................44 AP	Oven Tortilla Chips.................10 AP
Slow Cooker Wassail.............20 HF	Blue Cobb Dressing......................8 SA	Sesame Sticks ....11 AP

MOST LOVED COOKBOOKS KEY: Appetizers **AP** • Brunches **BR** • Casseroles **CA** • Cookies **CO** • Festive Baking **FB** • Holiday Favourites **HF**
Main Courses **MC** • Salads & Dressings **SA** • Slow Cooker Creations **SC** • Stir-fries **SF** • Summertime Desserts **SD** • Treats **TR**

6 recipes — most loved cookbooks compilation index

B to C

Toast Cups .... 31 AP
Toast Points .... 31 AP
Toast Squares .... 31 AP
Toast Triangles .... 31 AP
Tortilla Chips .... 10 AP
Tortilla Crisps .... 10 AP
Welsh Cakes .... 50 AP
Breads & Loaves
   Breads & Loaves, Banana
      Bread .... 20 BR
   Chocolate-Kissed Banana
      Bread .... 20 BR
   Coffee-Glazed Cinnamon
      Rolls .... 16 BR
   Feta Crescent Swirls .... 25 BR
   Fruity Almond Ring .... 18 BR
   Granola Banana Bread .... 20 BR
   Herb Bread Ring .... 12 BR
   Mincemeat Nut Bread .... 97 FB
   Poppy Seed Loaf .... 20 BR
   Savoury Cheese Rolls .... 14 BR
   Skinny Monkey Bread .... 20 BR
Breads & Quick Breads
   Batter-Ready Ginger Muffins ..... 8 HF
   Biscuit Fruit Roll .... 12 HF
   Breakfast Pull-Aparts .... 9 HF
   Cranberry Mint Loaf .... 118 HF
   Crisp Almond Pepper Bread .... 34 HF
   Easy Cinnamon Knots .... 10 HF
   Eggnog Candy Bread .... 119 HF
   Raspberry Cream Muffins .... 6 HF
   Stilton Puffs .... 32 HF
Breads, see Yeast Breads
Breakfast
   Batter-Ready Ginger Muffins ..... 8 HF
   Best Hash Browns .... 17 HF
   Biscuit Fruit Roll .... 12 HF
   Blueberry Streusel
      French Toast .... 14 HF
   Breakfast Pull-Aparts .... 9 HF

Easy Cinnamon Knots .... 10 HF
Make-Ahead Eggs Benedict ..... 16 HF
Pepper And Ham Strata .... 18 HF
Raspberry Cream Muffins .... 6 HF
Spiced Fruit Salad .... 13 HF
Breakfast Bars, Take-Along .... 98 TR
Breakfast Cookies, Take-Along .... 99 TR
Breakfast Pull-Aparts .... 9 HF
Breakfast Strata .... 40 BR
Breton Brittle .... 106 HF
Brie And Fruit Crostini,
   Grilled .... 36 AP
Brie In Pastry .... 35 AP
Brie Salad, Cranberry .... 44 SA
Brittle, Breton .... 106 HF
Brittle, Chocolate .... 100 TR
Broccoli Casserole .... 76 HF
Broccoli Casserole, Fresh .... 76 HF
Broccoli Salad .... 48 SA
Broccoli Shrimp Stir-Fry .... 66 SF
Broccoli Slaw .... 48 SA
Broccoli, Orange Beef And .... 24 SF
Broccoli, Spicy Beef And .... 26 SF
Broiled Herbed Rouladen .... 24 MC
Broiled Pineapple Chunks .... 32 SD
Broiled Salmon .... 54 MC
Broiled Steak, Zesty .... 24 MC
Broken Glass .... 66 SD
Broth, Scotch .... 15 SC
Brown Betty .... 27 FB
Brown Betty .... 71 TR
Brown Sugar And Spice .... 46 FB
Brownie Tart, Caramel .... 70 FB
Brownies, Blondie .... 60 FB
Brownies, Cream Cheese .... 62 FB
Brownies, Pudding .... 116 BR
Brownies, see Squares,
   Bars & Brownies
   Brunch Dish .... 47 BR
Bruschetta .... 90 AP

Brussels Sprouts, Sweet
   And Smoky .... 72 HF
Buffalo Wings .... 77 AP
Bulgogi .... 38 MC
Bundt Cake, Christmas .... 12 FB
Buns & Rolls
   Chocolate-Filled Rolls .... 108 FB
   Christmas Tree Buns .... 122 FB
   Easy Overnight Buns .... 106 FB
   Freezer Almond
      Cranberry Buns .... 110 FB
   Gingerbread Pull-Aparts .... 104 FB
   Knotty Cinnamon Buns .... 106 FB
Buns, French Toast Cinnamon .... 38 BR
Buried Cherry Balls .... 111 HF
Buried Cherry Balls .... 76 CO
Burnt Sugar Angel Food .... 38 SD
Burnt Sugar Syrup .... 38 SD
Burritos, Easy .... 102 SC
Butter Cookies, Cherry Almond ... 26 CO
Butter Cookies, Cherry Pecan ..... 26 CO
Butter Crust, Sweet .... 68 FB
Butter Lettuce Salad, Fruity .... 36 SA
Butter Tarts .... 74 FB
Butter Tarts .... 99 HF
Butter, Honey Mustard .... 22 MC
Butter, Onion .... 82 HF
Buttercream Icing, Almond .... 16 FB
Buttered Steak And Shrimp .... 22 MC
Butterflied Chicken .... 86 MC
Buttermilk Dressing .... 87 SA
Buttermilk Pancakes .... 28 BR
Butterscotch Confetti .... 81 TR
Butterscotch Cookies .... 30 CO
Butterscotch Cookies .... 51 TR
Butterscotch Muffins .... 116 TR
Butterscotch Shortbread .... 32 FB

C

Cabbage Roll Casserole, Lazy .... 19 CA
Cabbage Rolls .... 80 HF

MOST LOVED COOKBOOKS KEY: Appetizers **AP** • Brunches **BR** • Casseroles **CA** • Cookies **CO** • Festive Baking **FB** • Holiday Favourites **HF**
Main Courses **MC** • Salads & Dressings **SA** • Slow Cooker Creations **SC** • Stir-fries **SF** • Summertime Desserts **SD** • Treats **TR**

C

Cabbage Salad, Japanese ....52 SA	Festive Fruitcake ....6 FB	Cantonese Chicken .... 107 MC
Cacciatore Casserole ....58 CA	Fig And Pecan Cakes ....19 FB	Captain's Pie ....76 CA
Cacciatore, Chicken ....74 SC	Frozen Mocha Cheesecake ....86 SD	Caramel Apple Crisp ....28 FB
Caesar Croutons..........................28 SA	Honey Jewel Cake.................. 122 HF	Caramel Brownie Tart ....70 FB
Caesar Dressing, Creamy ....30 SA	Ice Cream Cake ....88 SD	Caramel Chocolate Squares ....63 FB
Caesar Dressing, Easy ....28 SA	Layered Gelato Cake ....90 SD	Caramel Corn, Special................60 AP
Caesar Dressing, Secret ....28 SA	Lazy Daisy ....8 TR	Caramel Filling ....70 FB
Caesar Salad................................28 SA	Lemon Coconut Angel ....39 SD	Caramel Fruit Dip.......................19 AP
Caesar Salad, Blackened	Lime Poppy Seed.....................10 TR	Caramel Hot Chocolate.................6 SC
Chicken ....30 SA	Mango Torte ....42 SD	Caramel Icing............................ 103 HF
Caesar, Sea Bass À La ....56 MC	Old-Fashioned Coffee Cake .. 110 BR	Caramel Icing..............................20 FB
Caesar, Secret..............................28 SA	Orange Chiffon Cake................40 SD	Caramel Kisses, Pecan ....31 TR
Caesar-Dressed Salad ....84 BR	Orange Chocolate Cake ....12 FB	Caramel Nut Pudding ....82 FB
Café Latté....................................10 BR	Orange, Yogurt And Poppy	Caramel Popcorn ....60 AP
Cajun Chicken.............................76 SC	Seed Cheesecake..................74 SD	Caramel Sauce ....18 SD
Cajun Seasoning ....62 MC	Pear Flower Gingerbread..........18 FB	Caramel Sauce ....66 TR
Cakes	Piña Colada Cake .... 108 BR	Caramel Sauce, Warm................80 FB
Almond And Raspberry	Pineapple Chiffon Cake .... 112 BR	Caramel Slice .... 103 HF
Cheesecake.....................72 SD	Rich Dark Fruitcake............... 120 HF	Caramelized Nuts..................... 112 AP
Angel Roll ....54 SD	Rum Cake ....24 FB	Caramelized Pears ....75 FB
Berry Mini-Cheesecakes........ 104 BR	Sticky Ginger Fig ....14 TR	Carrot Cookies ....12 CO
Black Forest Decadence...........14 FB	Strawberry Shortcake ....14 SD	Carrot Cream Cheese Roll .... 106 BR
Blueberry Coffee Cake........... 109 BR	Tri-Colour Angel Roll ....92 SD	Carrot Ginger Cookies................12 CO
Boiled Raisin Cake ....20 FB	Turtle Cheesecake ....10 FB	Carrot Onion Bake ....38 SC
Burnt Sugar Angel Food ....38 SD	Veggie Potato..........................94 BR	Carrot Salad ....50 SA
Carrot Cream Cheese Roll .... 106 BR	Vinarterta................................16 FB	Carrot Salad, Cranberry..............50 SA
Cheesy Cupcakes ....26 TR	White Chocolate Pound ....16 TR	Carrot Satay Soup ....16 SC
Chocolate Charlotte Russe.......46 SD	Camembert, Layered....................50 AP	Carrots, Cinnamon Honey ....76 HF
Chocolate Orange ....6 TR	Canapés	Carrots, Glazed Dill ....96 BR
Chocolate Raspberry	Cheesy Meat ....58 AP	Cashew Salad, Bean And............56 SA
Cheesecake.....................76 SD	Ham Roll ....34 AP	Cashew Vegetable Stir-Fry......... 110 SF
Chocolate Roulade Yule Log....88 HF	Salmon ....56 AP	Cashews, Tender Beef And............6 SF
Chocolate Truffle ....22 FB	Zippy ....58 AP	Casseroles
Christmas Bundt Cake ....12 FB	Candied Nuts ....24 HF	Barley And Rice Pilaf ....71 HF
Cream Cheese Delight .... 104 BR	Candies, see Sweets	Bev's Chicken .... 114 MC
Date ....12 TR	Candy Bar Cookies, Giant ....32 TR	Broccoli Casserole....................76 HF
Drumstick Cake ....84 SD	Candy Bar Squares ....92 TR	Festive Scalloped Potatoes.......70 HF
Dundee Cake..............................9 FB	Candy Bread, Eggnog .... 119 HF	Fresh Broccoli Casserole ....76 HF
Eggnog Cheesecake ....92 HF	Candy Cane Cookies....................45 TR	Marmalade-Glazed
Favourite Fruitcake ....8 FB	Cantaloupe Flan ....12 SD	Sweet Potatoes..................74 HF

MOST LOVED COOKBOOKS KEY: Appetizers **AP** • Brunches **BR** • Casseroles **CA** • Cookies **CO** • Festive Baking **FB** • Holiday Favourites **HF**
Main Courses **MC** • Salads & Dressings **SA** • Slow Cooker Creations **SC** • Stir-fries **SF** • Summertime Desserts **SD** • Treats **TR**

C

Sausage Stuffing Casserole .... 55 HF
Sweet Potato Casserole .... 75 HF
Turnip Cheese Casserole .... 74 HF
Wild Rice Stuffing Casserole .... 57 HF
Cassoulet .... 118 CA
Cauliflower Soup, Curried .... 21 SC
Celery Seed Dressing .... 54 SA
Celery Seed Slaw, Creamy .... 54 SA
Celery-Sauced Chops .... 110 SC
Cereal Cookies, Bran .... 24 CO
Champagne Orange Juice .... 6 BR
Chap Jae .... 34 SF
Charlotte Russe, Chocolate .... 46 SD
Checkerboard Shortbread .... 28 CO
Cheddar Tarts, Baby .... 97 AP
Cheese Ball, Best .... 28 HF
Cheese Ball, Festive Best .... 28 HF
Cheese Bites .... 84 AP
Cheese Casserole, Turnip .... 74 HF
Cheese Cubes .... 55 AP
Cheese Pie, Spinach .... 46 BR
Cheese Roll, Spinach And .... 72 BR
Cheese Rolls, Savoury .... 14 BR
Cheese Salad, Cherry .... 71 SA
Cheese Sauce .... 92 CA
Cheese Strata .... 102 CA
Cheese Tarts .... 56 AP
Cheese Thins .... 39 AP
Cheese, Cranberry .... 28 HF
Cheese, Macaroni And .... 86 CA
Cheesecakes
   Almond And Raspberry .... 72 SD
   Berry Mini- .... 104 BR
   Blue .... 44 AP
   Cherry Chilled .... 24 TR
   Chocolate Raspberry .... 76 SD
   Cookie .... 20 TR
   Crème de Menthe .... 22 TR
   Eggnog .... 92 HF
   Frozen Cheesecake Bites .... 113 TR

Frozen Mocha .... 86 SD
Mini-Chip .... 25 TR
Orange, Yogurt And
   Poppy Seed .... 74 SD
Pumpkin .... 18 TR
Turtle .... 10 FB
Cheesy Cupcakes .... 26 TR
Cheesy Fish Fillets .... 63 MC
Cheesy Meat Canapés .... 58 AP
Cheesy Pea Salad .... 50 SA
Chef's Dressing .... 6 SA
Chef's Salad .... 6 SA
Cherries, Chocolate .... 110 HF
Cherry Almond Butter Cookies ... 26 CO
Cherry Balls, Buried .... 111 HF
Cherry Balls, Buried .... 76 CO
Cherry Cheese Salad .... 71 SA
Cherry Chilled Cheesecake .... 24 TR
Cherry Coconut Macaroons .... 28 TR
Cherry Nanaimo Bars,
   Chocolate .... 100 HF
Cherry Pecan Butter Cookies ...... 26 CO
Cherry Pork Chops .... 109 SC
Cherry Shortbread, Nutty .... 99 CO
Cherry Slice, Chocolate .... 94 TR
Cherry Snacks .... 18 CO
Cherry Squares .... 88 TR
Cherry Strudel Dessert .... 24 FB
Cherry Winks .... 72 CO
Chewy Cookie Clusters .... 103 CO
Chicken
   Almond Chicken .... 58 SF
   Aniseed .... 108 MC
   Arroz Con Pollo .... 40 CA
   Asian Citrus Chicken .... 56 SF
   Bali Wings .... 76 AP
   Bev's Chicken Casserole ...... 114 MC
   Blackened .... 30 SA
   Blackened Chicken
      Caesar Salad .... 30 SA

Buffalo Wings .... 77 AP
Butterflied .... 86 MC
Cacciatore Casserole .... 58 CA
Cajun Chicken .... 76 SC
Cantonese .... 107 MC
Chicken 'N' Rice .... 42 CA
Chicken 'N' Stuffing .... 48 SF
Chicken And Black Bean
   Stir-Fry .... 52 SF
Chicken And Dumpling
   Soup .... 30 SC
Chicken And Greens .... 40 SF
Chicken and Leek Frittata .... 59 BR
Chicken And Stuffing Meal .... 79 SC
Chicken Cacciatore .... 74 SC
Chicken Chow Mein .... 44 SF
Chicken Divan .... 39 CA
Chicken Fajita Dinner .... 50 SF
Chicken Fried Rice .... 78 SF
Chicken Noodles Romanoff .... 56 CA
Chicken Parmigiana .... 84 SC
Chicken Pot Pie .... 48 CA
Chicken Pot Pie .... 66 BR
Chicken Supreme .... 38 SF
Chicken Tetrazzini .... 54 CA
Chicken Vegetable
   Fried Rice .... 64 SF
Cock-A-Leekie .... 28 SC
Coq Au Vin .... 72 SC
Coq Au Vin .... 98 MC
Corn And Bean-Stuffed
   Peppers .... 92 SC
Crispy .... 114 MC
Crustless Chicken Pie .... 46 CA
Crusty Parmesan Wings .... 80 AP
Curious Chicken Chili .... 91 SC
Curried Chicken Rolls .... 102 AP
Drumstick Bake .... 74 SC
Dumpling Casserole .... 50 CA
Easy Stir-Fry .... 54 SF

MOST LOVED COOKBOOKS KEY: Appetizers **AP** • Brunches **BR** • Casseroles **CA** • Cookies **CO** • Festive Baking **FB** • Holiday Favourites **HF**
Main Courses **MC** • Salads & Dressings **SA** • Slow Cooker Creations **SC** • Stir-fries **SF** • Summertime Desserts **SD** • Treats **TR**

C

Elegant .... 92 MC	Sweet Orange Chicken............ 42 SF	Chili Basil Dressing .... 65 SA
Glazed Wings .... 108 AP	Thai Pizza On A Garlic Crust.... 104 MC	Chili Black Beans .... 105 SC
Golden Glazed .... 111 MC	Uptown Asparagus Chicken .... 66 BR	Chili Cheese Log .... 43 AP
Handy Dandy Chicken .... 42 CA	Warm Chicken Salad .... 46 SA	Chili Con Queso........................... 42 AP
Holiday .... 116 MC	Yakitori .... 110 AP	Chili Dipping Sauce..................... 82 AP
Kung Pao............................... 102 MC	Chicken 'N' Rice....................... 42 CA	Chili Dressing .... 32, 92 SA
Kung Pao Chicken.................... 62 SF	Chicken 'N' Stuffing................. 48 SF	Chili Dressing, Sweet.................... 24 SA
Lettuce Wraps .... 86 AP	Chicken And Black Bean	Chili Garlic Dressing..................... 62 SA
Margo's Rosemary................... 90 MC	Stir-Fry.................................. 52 SF	Chili Lemon Shrimp .... 64 AP
Meatballs With Chutney	Chicken And Dumpling Soup ...... 30 SC	Chili Snacks, Green .... 119 AP
Sauce................................. 96 AP	Chicken And Greens................. 40 SF	Chili, Curious Chicken.................. 91 SC
Mediterranean Chicken	Chicken And Leek Frittata .... 59 BR	Chili, Pork And Pear Stir-Fry .... 93 SF
And Bean Casserole............ 44 CA	Chicken And Stuffing Meal .... 79 SC	Chilled Cheesecake, Cherry.......... 24 TR
Moroccan Chicken .... 88 SC	Chicken Cacciatore .... 74 SC	Chilled Chocolate Dessert .... 68 SD
Mushroom Chicken Sauce........ 90 SC	Chicken Chow Mein .... 44 SF	Chinese Chews............................. 59 FB
Orange Chicken .... 87 SC	Chicken Cordon Bleu .... 96 MC	Chinese Mushroom Soup............. 12 SC
Oriental Chicken Salad .... 52 SA	Chicken Diable .... 110 MC	Chinese Pepper Steak................... 52 SC
Oriental Rice Casserole .... 60 CA	Chicken Divan .... 39 CA	Chinese Stir-Fry
Oriental Wings .... 108 AP	Chicken Fajita Dinner .... 50 SF	Vegetables............................. 106 SF
Oven Cordon Bleu ....96 MC	Chicken Fried Rice.................... 78 SF	Chinese-Style Hash...................... 16 CA
Pan Cordon Bleu ....96 MC	Chicken Gravy......................... 84 MC	Chipper Muffins .... 116 TR
Parmesan Chicken	Chicken In Cream .... 111 MC	Chipper Pizza .... 16 CO
Drumettes .... 80 SC	Chicken Mole.......................... 93 MC	Chips
Parmesan Chicken Wings 80	Chicken Noodles Romanoff........ 56 CA	Minted Pita........................... 121 SA
Peanut Butter Chicken............. 82 SC	Chicken Parmesan.................... 89 MC	Oven Tortilla .... 10 AP
Peppered Chicken .... 60 SF	Chicken Parmigiana .... 84 SC	Tortilla .... 10 AP
Pineapple And Coconut .... 100 MC	Chicken Pot Pie .... 48 CA	Choco Cream Cheese Icing.......... 62 FB
Raspberry Chicken................... 84 SC	Chicken Pot Pie .... 66 BR	Choco-Cran Biscotti .... 66 CO
Rich Chicken Stew................... 86 SC	Chicken Supreme...................... 38 SF	Chocolate
Riviera Chicken Casserole .... 52 CA	Chicken Tetrazzini..................... 54 CA	Almond Fruit Bark .... 107 HF
Roast .... 84 MC	Chicken Vegetable Fried Rice .... 64 SF	Banana Split .... 110 SD
Sesame .... 106 MC	Chicken Veggie Crustless	Breton Brittle .... 106 HF
Sesame Chicken .... 41 SF	Quiche .... 42 BR	Chocolate Charlotte Russe....... 46 SD
Speedy .... 110 MC	Chickpea Tomato Salad .... 60 SA	Chocolate Cherries .... 110 HF
Spicy Balsamic Chicken .... 46 SF	Chiffon Cake, Orange .... 40 SD	Chocolate Cherry
Spring Rolls .... 88 AP	Chiffon Cake, Pineapple .... 112 BR	Nanaimo Bars................. 100 HF
Stuffed Breasts Of................... 88 MC	Chiffon Pie, Chocolate Mocha ..... 82 SD	Chocolate Mocha
Stuffed Chicken Rolls............... 78 SC	Chiffon Pie, Orange..................... 83 SD	Chiffon Pie.......................... 82 SD
Sweet And Sour Wings............ 81 AP	Chiffon, Lemon .... 52 SD	Chocolate Raspberry
Sweet Heat Peanut................. 92 MC	Chili .... 66 SC	Cheesecake....................... 76 SD

MOST LOVED COOKBOOKS KEY: Appetizers **AP** • Brunches **BR** • Casseroles **CA** • Cookies **CO** • Festive Baking **FB** • Holiday Favourites **HF** • Main Courses **MC** • Salads & Dressings **SA** • Slow Cooker Creations **SC** • Stir-fries **SF** • Summertime Desserts **SD** • Treats **TR**

C

Chocolate Roulade
    Yule Log .... 88 HF
Drumstick Cake .... 84 SD
Five-Minute Fudge .... 108 HF
Frozen Fudge Pops .... 109 SD
Frozen Mocha Cheesecake ...... 86 SD
Grasshopper Pie .... 80 SD
Ice Cream Sandwiches .... 96 SD
Macadamia Tortoni .... 114 SD
Mud Pie .... 108 SD
Orange Chocolate Squares ... 104 HF
Peppermint Nanaimo Bars ... 100 HF
Rum Balls .... 112 HF
Sundae Dessert .... 98 SD
Swirl Ice Cream With
    Grilled Cake And Berries ..... 48 SD
White Chocolate
    Fudge Truffles .... 112 HF
White Chocolate
    Ice Cream .... 112 SD
White Chocolate
    Orange Chill .... 87 SD
Chocolate And Pear Muffins .... 21 BR
Chocolate Banana Bread .... 94 FB
Chocolate Biscotti, Mandarin .... 48 FB
Chocolate Brittle .... 100 TR
Chocolate Cake, Orange .... 12 FB
Chocolate Charlotte Russe .... 46 SD
Chocolate Cherries .... 110 HF
Chocolate Cherry
    Naniamo Bars .... 100 HF
Chocolate Cherry Slice .... 94 TR
Chocolate Chippers .... 16 CO
Chocolate Chippers, Decadent ..... 16 CO
Chocolate Coconut Melts .... 98 TR
Chocolate Coffee Icing .... 96 TR
Chocolate Cookies, Boiled .... 94 CO
Chocolate Crinkles .... 64 CO
Chocolate Crisps .... 74 TR
Chocolate Crumb Crust .... 22 TR
Chocolate Crust .... 22 FB
Chocolate Cups .... 114 SD
Chocolate Dips .... 66 TR
Chocolate Eggnog Pudding .... 78 FB
Chocolate Filling .... 42 FB
Chocolate Filling, Cool .... 122 CO
Chocolate Fudge Sauce .... 66 TR
Chocolate Glaze .... 22 FB
Chocolate Glaze, White .... 13 FB
Chocolate Icing .... 14 CO
Chocolate Marshmallows .... 102 TR
Chocolate Minis, Double- .... 60 FB
Chocolate Mints, Fudgy .... 122 TR
Chocolate Mocha Chiffon Pie ...... 82 SD
Chocolate Mousse .... 56 TR
Chocolate Nuggets .... 19 CO
Chocolate Nuts .... 102 TR
Chocolate Orange Cake .... 6 TR
Chocolate Orange Icing .... 6 TR
Chocolate Peanut Drops .... 90 CO
Chocolate Pinwheels .... 34 CO
Chocolate Raspberry
    Cheesecake .... 76 SD
Chocolate Roll .... 84 TR
Chocolate Roulade Yule Log .... 88 HF
Chocolate Sandwiches .... 41 FB
Chocolate Shortbread, Rolled .... 102 CO
Chocolate Softies .... 14 CO
Chocolate Sour Cream
    Topping .... 22 TR
Chocolate Spritz .... 83 CO
Chocolate Squares, Caramel .... 63 FB
Chocolate Tom Thumbs .... 42 FB
Chocolate Truffle .... 22 FB
Chocolate, Caramel Hot .... 6 SC
Chocolate-Dipped Lemon
    Cookies .... 36 CO
Chocolate-Dipped Nutty
    Biscotti .... 67 CO
Chocolate-Filled Rolls .... 108 FB
Chocolate-Kissed Banana Bread ... 20 BR
Choco-Peanut Fudge .... 108 TR
Chop-Chop Teriyaki Tofu .... 114 SF
Chops
    Barbecued Flavoured Pork .... 70 MC
    Best Pork .... 70 MC
    Celery-Sauced .... 110 SC
    Cherry Pork .... 109 SC
    Lamb .... 82 MC
    Normandy, Pork .... 110 SC
    Orange Pork .... 72 MC
Chow Mein, Chicken .... 44 SF
Chow Mein, Shrimp .... 44 SF
Chowder, Lobster .... 39 HF
Chowder, Manhattan Clam .... 18 SC
Christmas Bread .... 118 FB
Christmas Bundt Cake .... 12 FB
Christmas Cookies .... 110 CO
Christmas Cranapple Pies .... 96 HF
Christmas Punch .... 20 HF
Christmas Spirit .... 23 HF
Christmas Tree Buns .... 122 FB
Chunky Vegetable Salad .... 40 SA
Chunky Zucchini Soup .... 20 SC
Chutney Sauce .... 96 AP
Chutney Sauce, Meatballs With ... 96 AP
Cider Dressing .... 88 SA
Cider Vinaigrette, Apple .... 110 SA
Cinnamon Brandy Sauce .... 14 TR
Cinnamon Buns, French Toast ..... 38 BR
Cinnamon Buns, Knotty .... 106 FB
Cinnamon Honey .... 76 HF
Cinnamon Honey Carrots .... 76 HF
Cinnamon Knots, Easy .... 10 HF
Cinnamon Roll Cookies .... 38 CO
Cinnamon Rolls, Coffee-Glazed ... 16 BR
Citrus Chicken, Asian .... 56 SF
Citrus Punch, Pineapple .... 8 BR
Clam Chowder, Manhattan .... 18 SC
Cloverleaf Shortbread .... 28 CO

MOST LOVED COOKBOOKS KEY: Appetizers **AP** • Brunches **BR** • Casseroles **CA** • Cookies **CO** • Festive Baking **FB** • Holiday Favourites **HF** • Main Courses **MC** • Salads & Dressings **SA** • Slow Cooker Creations **SC** • Stir-fries **SF** • Summertime Desserts **SD** • Treats **TR**

C

Clusters, Chewy Cookie .... 103 CO
Coating, Cornmeal .... 56 MC
Coating, Graham Cracker .... 92 CO
Coating, Steak With Spice .... 20 MC
Cobb Dressing, Blue .... 8 SA
Cobb Salad .... 8 SA
Cobbler, Peachy Rhubarb .... 10 SD
Cobblers, see Crisps & Cobblers
Cock-A-Leekie .... 28 SC
Cocktail Sauce, Homemade ...... 13 AP
Cocktail, Shrimp .... 115 AP
Cocktail, Shrimp .... 38 HF
Coconut
    Apricot Balls .... 92 CO
    Best Drop Cookies .... 6 CO
    Cherry Snacks .... 18 CO
    Chipper Pizza .... 16 CO
    Crackerjack Cookies .... 76 CO
    Cream Cheese Balls .... 92 CO
    Macaroons .... 22 CO
    Raspberry Pinwheels .... 34 CO
    Spicy Dads .... 11 CO
    Strawberry Cream Cookies .... 80 CO
    Striped Corners .... 106 CO
    Toffee Cookies .... 86 CO
Coconut Angel, Lemon .... 39 SD
Coconut Chicken,
    Pineapple And .... 100 MC
Coconut Cookies .... 44 CO
Coconut Cream Pie .... 79 SD
Coconut Diagonals .... 44 TR
Coconut Ice Cream, Vanilla ..... 112 SD
Coconut Macaroons, Cherry ..... 28 TR
Coconut Melts, Chocolate .... 98 TR
Coconut Meringues, Pineapple .. 43 SD
Coconut Peaks .... 41 TR
Coconut Rum Diagonals .... 44 TR
Coconut Salsa, Papaya .... 20 MC
Coconut Shrimp .... 85 AP
Coconut Topping .... 44 CO

Coconut Topping .... 58 FB
Coconut Topping .... 8 TR
Coffee Balls, Glazed .... 88 CO
Coffee Cake, Blueberry .... 109 BR
Coffee Cake, Old-Fashioned .... 110 BR
Coffee Fingers .... 46 CO
Coffee Glaze .... 12 HF
Coffee Glaze .... 16 BR
Coffee Glaze .... 88 CO
Coffee Icing, Chocolate .... 96 TR
Coffee Meringues .... 82 CO
Coffee, Special Spiced .... 10 BR
Coffee-Glazed Cinnamon Rolls . 16 BR
Coleslaw, Orange Poppy Seed .. 86 BR
Coleslaw, Overnight .... 54 SA
Comfort Roast .... 60 HF
Company Meatloaf .... 43 MC
Confetti Beans .... 78 HF
Cooked Salad Dressing .... 106 SA
Cookie Cheesecake .... 20 TR
Cookie Crumb Crust .... 20 TR
Cookie Cups .... 60 CO
Cookie Ornaments .... 114 CO
Cookie Pizza .... 36 TR
Cookies, see Bars & Cookies
Cookies
    Basic Sugar Cookies .... 38 FB
    Brown Sugar And Spice .... 46 FB
    Butterscotch .... 51 TR
    Butterscotch Shortbread .... 32 FB
    Candy Cane .... 45 TR
    Cherry Coconut Macaroons .. 28 TR
    Chocolate Sandwiches .... 41 FB
    Chocolate Tom Thumbs .... 42 FB
    Coconut Diagonals .... 44 TR
    Coconut Peaks .... 41 TR
    Coconut Rum Diagonals .... 44 TR
    Cranberry Almond Biscotti .... 49 FB
    Cranberry Chip .... 30 TR
    Fruit Scrolls .... 35 FB

Giant Candy Bar .... 32 TR
Gingerbread Stars .... 30 FB
Hermits .... 50 TR
Icebox Ribbons .... 40 TR
Lebkuchen .... 44 FB
Mandarin Chocolate Biscotti ... 48 FB
Mincemeat Bites .... 34 FB
Mincemeat Puffs .... 36 FB
Noodle Power .... 41 TR
Nutri- .... 48 TR
Oatmeal Chip .... 37 TR
Peanut Butter Hide-Aways .... 36 TR
Pecan Caramel Kisses .... 31 TR
Rainbow Chip .... 38 TR
Santa's Whiskers .... 45 FB
Shortbread .... 32 FB
Soft Molasses Drops .... 49 TR
Stollen Tea Dunkers .... 50 FB
Sugar .... 46 TR
Swedish Tea Cakes .... 34 TR
Swirling Dervish Cookies .... 40 FB
Take-Along Breakfast .... 99 TR
Whipped Shortbread .... 44 TR
Cool Chocolate Filling .... 122 CO
Cool Fruit Dip .... 35 SD
Coq Au Vin .... 72 SC
Coq Au Vin .... 98 MC
Cordon Bleu
    Chicken .... 96 MC
    Oven .... 96 MC
    Pan .... 96 MC
Corn And Bean-Stuffed
    Peppers .... 92 SC
Corn And Tomato Salad .... 24 SA
Corn Pudding .... 97 BR
Corn Salad, Creamy .... 64 SA
Corned Beef Dinner .... 50 SC
Corned Beef Hash .... 64 BR
Corned Beef Mousse .... 30 AP
Cornish Hens .... 118 MC

MOST LOVED COOKBOOKS KEY: Appetizers **AP** • Brunches **BR** • Casseroles **CA** • Cookies **CO** • Festive Baking **FB** • Holiday Favourites **HF**
Main Courses **MC** • Salads & Dressings **SA** • Slow Cooker Creations **SC** • Stir-fries **SF** • Summertime Desserts **SD** • Treats **TR**

C

Cornmeal Coating......................56 MC
Cornmeal Flatbread With
   Spinach And Onions................92 AP
Cornmeal-Crusted Salmon............56 MC
Corny Shepherd's Pie..................116 SC
Coulibiac....................................64 HF
Couscous Salad, Cucumber And ..92 SA
Couscous, Lemon Cranberry......102 BR
Couscous, Vegetable..................118 SF
Crab Ball, Sauced........................12 AP
Crab Dip, Hot..............................16 AP
Crab Mousse...............................32 AP
Crab Salad, Parfait......................18 SA
Crab Tartlets..............................122 AP
Crab Tarts...................................36 HF
Crab, Crepes À La.......................26 BR
Crabapple Meatballs...................37 HF
Crackerjack Cookies....................76 CO
Crackles, Lemon..........................74 CO
Cranapple Pies, Christmas...........96 HF
Cranapple Tarts...........................72 FB
Cranberry Almond Bark............103 TR
Cranberry Almond Biscotti..........49 FB
Cranberry Apple Warmer...............6 SC
Cranberry Brie Salad...................44 SA
Cranberry Buns,
   Freezer Almond.....................110 FB
Cranberry Carrot Salad................50 SA
Cranberry Cheese........................28 HF
Cranberry Chip Cookies..............30 TR
Cranberry Couscous, Lemon.....102 BR
Cranberry Dressing......................45 SA
Cranberry Jelly Salad...................68 SA
Cranberry Macadamia
   Mounds..................................112 CO
Cranberry Meatballs..................100 AP
Cranberry Mint Loaf..................118 HF
Cranberry Mulled Wine...............10 SC
Cranberry Pecan Bread..............114 FB
Cranberry Pie..............................64 FB

Cranberry Sauce..........................42 SC
Cranberry Sauce..........................55 HF
Cranberry Sparkle Muffins...........84 FB
Cranberry Stuffing, Spiced........122 MC
Cranberry Wedges, Orange.........91 FB
Cranberry White Chocolate
   Cookies....................................58 CO
Cranberry, Ham With..................78 MC
Cranberry, Hot Buttered..............10 SC
Cranberry, Hot Spiced.................10 SC
Cran-Raspberry Ice...................116 SD
Cream Cheese Balls....................92 CO
Cream Cheese Brownies.............62 FB
Cream Cheese Brownies.............96 TR
Cream Cheese Cookies...............30 CO
Cream Cheese Crescents............31 CO
Cream Cheese Danish
   Pastries..................................102 FB
Cream Cheese Delight..............104 BR
Cream Cheese Icing, Choco........62 FB
Cream Cheese Pastry..................36 HF
Cream Cheese Pastry..........66, 97 AP
Cream Cheese Roll, Carrot........106 BR
Cream Cheese Tea Ring............100 FB
Cream Layers, Strawberry...........14 SD
Cream Pie, Banana......................63 SD
Cream Pie, Coconut....................79 SD
Cream Quesadillas, Apple...........22 SD
Cream Sauce, Mushroom..........112 CA
Cream Scones.............................93 FB
Cream, Chicken In....................111 MC
Cream, Maple Orange
   Whipped..................................98 HF
Cream, Peaches And...................64 SD
Cream, Peaches And...................78 BR
Creamed Spinach........................98 BR
Creamed Turkey Noodle..............62 CA
Creamy Caesar Dressing.............30 SA
Creamy Celery Seed Slaw...........54 SA
Creamy Corn Salad.....................64 SA

Creamy Dill Dressing..................44 SA
Creamy Dressing.........................50 SA
Creamy Dressing, Sweet.............48 SA
Creamy Garlic Dressing............108 SA
Creamy Greek Bake....................10 CA
Creamy Horseradish Dressing.......66 SA
Creamy Horseradish Sauce.........60 HF
Creamy Ice Pops.......................109 SD
Creamy Lemon Dressing.............16 SA
Creamy Mint Dressing................96 SA
Creamy Mustard Dressing...........50 SA
Creamy Zucchini Wedges...........48 BR
Crème de Menthe
   Cheesecake.............................22 TR
Creole
   Beef..116 CA
   Lamb......................................116 CA
   Shrimp.....................................77 SF
Crepes
   Basic Crepes............................26 BR
   Crepes À La Crab.....................26 BR
   Savoury Crepes........................26 BR
   Wheat Crepes..........................26 BR
Crepes À La Crab........................26 BR
Crescent Swirls, Feta...................25 BR
Crinkles, Chocolate.....................64 CO
Crisp Almond Pepper Bread........34 HF
Crisps & Cobblers
   Brown Betty.............................27 FB
   Caramel Apple Crisp................28 FB
   Chocolate Crisps......................74 TR
   Fruit Cobbler............................26 FB
   PBJ Crisps................................32 CO
   Raisin Cobbler.........................28 FB
   Rhubarb Crisp........................114 BR
   Tortilla Crisps..........................10 AP
Crispy Chicken.........................114 MC
Crispy Cukes..............................60 SA
Crispy Roll................................112 TR
Croissant Pudding, Apple............83 FB

MOST LOVED COOKBOOKS KEY: Appetizers **AP** • Brunches **BR** • Casseroles **CA** • Cookies **CO** • Festive Baking **FB** • Holiday Favourites **HF**
Main Courses **MC** • Salads & Dressings **SA** • Slow Cooker Creations **SC** • Stir-fries **SF** • Summertime Desserts **SD** • Treats **TR**

most loved cookbooks compilation index — recipes 13

C to D

Croissant Strawberry Pudding... 114 BR
Crostini, Grilled Brie And Fruit... 36 AP
Croutons
   Basil Pesto .... 120 SA
   Caesar .... 28 SA
   Tomato Pesto .... 120 SA
Croutons .... 43 SA
Croutons .... 82 BR
Crunchies .... 71 AP
Crunchy Rice Salad .... 102 SA
Crunchy Vegetable Macaroni....... 88 CA
Crustless Chicken Pie................. 46 CA
Crusts
   Chocolate Crumb................. 22 TR
   Chocolate Crust................... 22 FB
   Cookie Crumb....................... 20 TR
   Gingersnap Crumb................ 18 TR
   Graham Crumb .... 24, 60, 61 TR
   Meringue................................ 56 SD
   Nutty Shortbread .... 64 SD
   Pecan .... 102 SD
   Processor Pecan Pastry .... 70 FB
   Shortbread .... 51, 62,100 SD
   Shortbread .... 58 FB
   Shortcrust Pastry .... 67 FB
   Sugary Pizza .... 6 SD
   Sweet Butter Crust .... 68 FB
   Vanilla Wafer .... 92 HF
   Walnut Crust .... 66 FB
Crusty Parmesan Wings................ 80 AP
Cucumber And
   Couscous Salad .... 92 SA
Cucumber Avocado Salad .... 16 SA
Cucumber Dill Salad .... 80 BR
Cucumber Dressing................... 116 SA
Cucumber Mousse..................... 80 BR
Cucumber Salad, Layered .... 72 SA
Cucumber Salad, Perfect............. 72 SA
Cucumber Sour Cream Salad...... 72 SA
Cucumbers In Sour Cream........... 58 SA

Cuke Spread 'R Dip.................... 22 AP
Cukes, Crispy .... 60 SA
Cupcakes, Cheesy .... 26 TR
Cups, Chocolate....................... 114 SD
Cups, Cookie .... 60 CO
Cups, Dirt................................. 60 CO
Curious Chicken Chili................. 91 SC
Currant Scones.......................... 90 FB
Curried Cauliflower Soup .... 21 SC
Curried Chicken Rolls .... 102 AP
Curried Pork And
   Mango Sauce .... 88 SF
Curry
   Fruity Beef .... 10 SF
   Shrimp Mango .... 64 MC
   Slow Cooker Lamb .... 118 SC
   Vegetable .... 100 SC
Curry Dip, Seafood.................... 30 HF
Curry Hotpot, Beef..................... 54 SC
Curry Vinaigrette...................... 100 SA
Custard .... 18 SD
Custard, Lemon Sponge .... 120 BR
Custard, Orange .... 26 SD
Cutlets In Wine Sauce, Veal......... 50 MC

Danish Pastries .... 102 FB
Danish Pastries,
   Cream Cheese .... 102 FB
Date And Blue Cheese Tarts...... 106 AP
Date Bars, Orange.................... 116 BR
Date Cake .... 12 TR
Date Filling .... 86 TR
Date Pinwheels.......................... 34 CO
Date Pudding, Sticky.................. 80 FB
Dates
   Best Drop Cookies................... 6 CO
   Cherry Snacks....................... 18 CO
   Cherry Winks........................ 72 CO
   Christmas Cookies................ 110 CO
   Fruitcake Cookies................. 104 CO

Hermits...................................... 8 CO
Merry Fruit Cookies .... 96 CO
Death By Chocolate .... 54 TR
Decadent Chocolate Chippers .....16 CO
Desserts
   Baked Apples........................ 70 TR
   Banana Macadamia
      Sundaes.......................... 66 TR
   Berry Mini-Cheesecakes........ 104 BR
   Blueberry Coffee Cake.......... 109 BR
   Blueberry Lemon Trifle .... 122 BR
   Bocconne Dolce .... 52 TR
   Brandied Peaches .... 70 TR
   Brown Betty .... 71 TR
   Carrot Cream Cheese Roll .... 106 BR
   Cherry Strudel Dessert........... 24 HF
   Chocolate Mousse................. 56 TR
   Cream Cheese Delight .... 104 BR
   Croissant Strawberry
      Pudding........................ 114 BR
   Death By Chocolate .... 54 TR
   Fresh Fruit Betty .... 71 TR
   Fruit Pizza............................. 62 TR
   Glimmering Slice................... 61 TR
   Lemon Meringue Squares..... 118 BR
   Lemon Sponge Custard........ 120 BR
   Mango Raspberry Trifles....... 56 TR
   Mocha Mousse.................... 121 BR
   Old-Fashioned
      Coffee Cake .... 110 BR
   Orange Date Bars................ 116 BR
   Peanut Ice Cream Treat......... 64 TR
   Piña Colada Cake .... 108 BR
   Pineapple Chiffon Cake .... 112 BR
   Poached Maple Pears .... 68 TR
   Pudding Brownies .... 116 BR
   Raisin Bread Pudding............ 86 HF
   Raspberry .... 60 TR
   Rhubarb Betty .... 71 TR
   Rhubarb Crisp .... 114 BR

MOST LOVED COOKBOOKS KEY: Appetizers **AP** • Brunches **BR** • Casseroles **CA** • Cookies **CO** • Festive Baking **FB** • Holiday Favourites **HF**
Main Courses **MC** • Salads & Dressings **SA** • Slow Cooker Creations **SC** • Stir-fries **SF** • Summertime Desserts **SD** • Treats **TR**

D

Sex In A Pan .... 58 TR
Sherry Trifle .... 90 HF
Six Layer .... 58 TR
Steamed Fruit Pudding .... 84 HF
Strawberry Meringue
    Shortcake .... 52 TR
Tropical Marshmallow
    Squares .... 117 BR
Truffle Trifle .... 54 TR
Devil's Dip .... 12 AP
Devil's Dip, Double .... 12 AP
Devilled Eggs .... 59 AP
Diamonds, Mocha .... 108 CO
Diced Tofu And Noodles .... 112 SF
Dijon Beef Stew .... 49 SC
Dijon Dressing .... 107 SA
Dill Carrots, Glazed .... 96 BR
Dill Dressing .... 80 BR
Dill Dressing, Creamy .... 44 SA
Dill Dressing, Lemon .... 56 SA
Dill Pasta Salad .... 90 BR
Dill Salad, Cucumber .... 80 BR
Dill Salmon, Orange And .... 54 MC
Dilled Snacks, Little .... 120 SA
Dilled Snapper Fry .... 76 SF
Dilly Beef Dinner .... 53 SC
Dilly Dip .... 17 AP
Dim Sum, Beefy Pepper .... 104 AP
Dips
    Antipasto .... 46 AP
    Apricot Sauce .... 122 AP
    Artichoke .... 28 AP
    Best Vegetable .... 14 AP
    Black Bean .... 8 AP
    Caramel Fruit .... 19 AP
    Chili Con Queso .... 42 AP
    Chili Dipping Sauce .... 82 AP
    Chocolate .... 66 TR
    Cool Fruit .... 35 SD
    Cuke Spread 'R .... 22 AP

Devil's .... 12 AP
Dilly .... 17 AP
Double Devil's .... 12 AP
Easy Fruit .... 19 AP
Fruity Salsa .... 36 AP
Homemade Cocktail Sauce ..... 13 AP
Hot Crab .... 16 AP
Hot Mushroom .... 40 AP
Kidney Bean .... 8 AP
King Artichoke .... 30 HF
Mint Papaya Salsa .... 25 AP
Peanut Butter .... 19 AP
Quick Salsa .... 48 AP
Refried Bean .... 52 AP
Seafood Curry .... 30 HF
Soy Fire .... 28 AP
Spicy Dipping Sauce .... 16 AP
Spinach .... 26 AP
Spreading Forest Fire .... 38 AP
Yogurt Fruit .... 34 SD
Dips & Spreads, Hot
    Artichoke Dip .... 28 AP
    Brie In Pastry .... 35 AP
    Chili Con Queso .... 42 AP
    Devil's Dip .... 12 AP
    Double Devil's Dip .... 12 AP
    Grilled Brie And
        Fruit Crostini .... 36 AP
    Hot Crab Dip .... 16 AP
    Hot Mushroom Dip .... 40 AP
    Kidney Bean Dip .... 8 AP
    Spinach Dip #1 .... 26 AP
    Spinach Dip #2 .... 26 AP
    Spreading Forest Fire .... 38 AP
Dirt Cups .... 60 CO
Dirt Filling .... 60 CO
Divan, Chicken .... 39 CA
Dolmades .... 62 AP
Dolmades, Slow Cooker .... 34 SC
Double Devil's Dip .... 12 AP

Double-Chocolate Minis .... 60 FB
Dressed Red Potatoes .... 36 SC
Dressings
    Apple Spice .... 38 SA
    Apricot .... 78 SA
    Asian .... 52 SA
    Balsamic .... 42 SA
    Balsamic .... 84 BR
    Basil .... 43 SA
    Basil Mustard .... 61 SA
    Blue Cheese .... 107 SA
    Blue Cobb .... 8 SA
    Buttermilk .... 87 SA
    Celery Seed .... 54 SA
    Chef's .... 6 SA
    Chili .... 32, 92 SA
    Chili Basil .... 65 SA
    Chili Garlic .... 62 SA
    Cider .... 88 SA
    Cooked Salad .... 106 SA
    Cranberry .... 45 SA
    Creamy .... 50 SA
    Creamy Caesar .... 30 SA
    Creamy Dill .... 44 SA
    Creamy Garlic .... 108 SA
    Creamy Horseradish .... 66 SA
    Creamy Lemon .... 16 SA
    Creamy Mint .... 96 SA
    Creamy Mustard .... 50 SA
    Cucumber .... 116 SA
    Dijon .... 107 SA
    Dill .... 80 BR
    Easy Caesar .... 28 SA
    French .... 106 SA
    Ginger .... 112 SA
    Greek .... 12 SA
    Green Goddess .... 34 SA
    Honey Mustard .... 116 SA
    Italian .... 104 SA
    Lemon Dill .... 56 SA

MOST LOVED COOKBOOKS KEY: Appetizers **AP** • Brunches **BR** • Casseroles **CA** • Cookies **CO** • Festive Baking **FB** • Holiday Favourites **HF**
Main Courses **MC** • Salads & Dressings **SA** • Slow Cooker Creations **SC** • Stir-fries **SF** • Summertime Desserts **SD** • Treats **TR**

D to E

Lemon Garlic..................46 SA
Light Lemon....................26 SA
Lime................................102 SA
Martini............................108 SA
Mustard...........................17 SA
Orange............................36 SA
Orange Poppy Seed........86 BR
Orange Poppy Seed........44 HF
Parsley Pesto...................82 SA
Peanut..............................90 SA
Pesto................................80 SA
Pink.................................111 SA
Poppy Seed....................110 SA
Poppy Seed......................87 BR
Raspberry.......................114 SA
Redcurrant......................82 BR
Sassy Salsa.......................22 SA
Secret Caesar..................28 SA
Sesame Soy...................112 SA
Simple Mayonnaise.........27 SA
Sour Cream.....................20 SA
Soy...................................66 SA
Spicy Ranch....................64 SA
Strawberry......................14 SA
Sweet Chili.....................24 SA
Sweet Creamy................48 SA
Sweet Veggie.................40 SA
Tangy Orange...............114 SA
Thousand Island...........117 SA
Warm Bacon...................34 SA
Drop Cookies
Best....................................6 CO
Bran Cereal Cookies......24 CO
Carrot Cookies...............12 CO
Carrot Ginger Cookies...12 CO
Cherry Snacks................18 CO
Chewy Cookie Clusters..103 CO
Chocolate Chippers........16 CO
Chocolate Chippers,
  Decadent......................16 CO

Chocolate Nuggets.........19 CO
Chocolate Peanut Drops..90 CO
Chocolate Softies............14 CO
Christmas Cookies.........110 CO
Cranberry Macadamia
  Mounds......................112 CO
Fruitcake Cookies.........104 CO
Gumdrop Cookies..........22 CO
Halloween Black Moons..122 CO
Hermits..............................8 CO
Macaroons......................22 CO
Mud Monsters..............122 CO
Oatmeal Raisin Cookies..18 CO
Pumpkin Cookies...........10 CO
Spicy Dads......................11 CO
Whipped Shortbread....102 CO
White Chip Cookies.......24 CO
Drumettes, Parmesan Chicken..80 SC
Drumstick Bake..............74 SC
Drumstick Cake..............84 SD
Drunken Watermelon....25 SD
Duck With Plum Sauce..116 MC
Dumplings......................16 SD
Dumplings......................99 SC
Dumplings
  Casserole.....................50 CA
  Dessert, Berry Rhubarb..16 SD
  Rosemary....................30 SC
  Soup, Chicken And.....30 SC
  Squash And................98 SC
  Sweet Potato..............50 CA
Dundee Cake....................9 FB

Easiest Ribs..................112 SC
Easy Burritos...............102 SC
Easy Caesar Dressing....28 SA
Easy Cinnamon Knots...10 HF
Easy Eggs Benny............50 BR
Easy Fruit Dip................19 AP
Easy Glaze......................46 TR

Easy Lemon Pepper.......88 CA
Easy Overnight Buns...106 FB
Easy Peanut Butter Cookies..58 CO
Easy Shepherd's Pie......25 CA
Easy Stir-Fry..................54 SF
Egg And Parsley Sauce..66 HF
Egg Nests.......................62 CO
Eggnog Candy Bread...119 HF
Eggnog Cheesecake.......92 HF
Eggnog Loaf, Orange....94 FB
Eggnog Muffins, Rummy..87 FB
Eggnog Pudding, Chocolate..78 FB
Eggnog Sauce................78 FB
Eggnog, Party................24 HF
Eggplant Parmigiana....94 CA
Eggplant Pasta Bake......96 CA
Eggs
  Asparagus Omelette...54 BR
  Make-Ahead Eggs
    Benedict..................16 HF
  Breakfast Strata..........40 BR
  Brunch Dish................47 BR
  Chicken And Leek Frittata..59 BR
  Chicken Veggie Crustless
    Quiche.....................42 BR
  Creamy Zucchini Wedges..48 BR
  Devilled......................59 AP
  Easy Eggs Benny.......50 BR
  Eggs Florentine..........50 BR
  Fiesta Strata...............39 BR
  Impossible Quiche.....44 BR
  Oven Scrambled Eggs..52 BR
  Pea And Shrimp Frittata
    Muffins....................58 BR
  Ribbon Zucchini Frittata..60 BR
  Scrambled Breakfast..52 BR
  Seafood Quiche..........42 BR
  Spinach And Bacon
    Omelette.................56 BR
  Spinach Cheese Pie....46 BR

MOST LOVED COOKBOOKS KEY: Appetizers **AP** • Brunches **BR** • Casseroles **CA** • Cookies **CO** • Festive Baking **FB** • Holiday Favourites **HF**
Main Courses **MC** • Salads & Dressings **SA** • Slow Cooker Creations **SC** • Stir-fries **SF** • Summertime Desserts **SD** • Treats **TR**

F

Tomato Basil Pie ....44 BR
Eggs Benedict,
   Make-Ahead ....16 HF
Eggs Florentine......................50 BR
Electric Grill, see Grilling
Elegant Chicken ....92 MC
Enchiladas, Mexican................64 BR
Enchiladas, Seafood................84 CA
Entrees
   Apricot Pork Loin Roast ....58 HF
   Comfort Roast ....60 HF
   Coulibiac ....64 HF
   French Tourtière ....63 HF
   Redcurrant And
      Mustard-Glazed Ham ....50 HF
   Roast Turkey ....52 HF
   Triple Seafood Noodles ....67 HF
   Turkey À La King ....47 HF
   Turkey Pies ....48 HF

Fajita Dinner, Chicken ....50 SF
Fajitas, Slow Cooker ....64 SC
Favourite Fruitcake ....8 FB
Favourite Mushrooms............ 114 AP
Fennel Parcels, Fish And ....60 MC
Festive Best Cheese Ball.........28 HF
Festive Fruit 'N' Nut Loaf ....96 FB
Festive Fruitcake ....6 FB
Festive Scalloped Potatoes......70 HF
Feta Crescent Swirls ....25 BR
Feta, Marinated .... 122 SA
Fiesta Strata.........................39 BR
Fig And Pecan Cakes ....19 FB
Fig Cake, Sticky Ginger ....14 TR
Filbert Fingers.......................71 CO
Filet Mignon
   Tournados ....28 MC
Filet, Acapulco Beef ....25 MC
Fillets, Cheesy Fish ....63 MC

Fillings
   Almond ....50 CO
   Almond ....68 FB
   Apricot ....89 TR
   Bourbon ....52 CO
   Caramel...............................70 FB
   Chocolate.............................42 FB
   Cool Chocolate .... 122 CO
   Date ....86 TR
   Dirt ....60 CO
   Lemon ....84 CO
   Lemon ....90 TR
   Mushroom ....66 AP
   Raisin .... 48, 118 CO
   Raisin ....66 FB
   Strawberry..........................80 CO
Finger Cookies, Almond ....119 CO
Fingers
   Coffee.................................46 CO
   Filbert ....71 CO
   Witch's .... 119 CO
Fire Dip, Soy........................28 AP
Fish & Seafood
   Antipasto ....27 HF
   Antipasto ....46 AP
   Baked Salmon ....70 BR
   Beef Oscar ....16 MC
   Black Bean Shrimp Noodles ....82 SF
   Blackened Snapper...............62 MC
   Broccoli Shrimp Stir-Fry ....66 SF
   Broiled Salmon ....54 MC
   Buttered Steak And Shrimp .....22 MC
   Captain's Pie........................76 CA
   Cheesy Fish Fillets................63 MC
   Chili Lemon Shrimp ....64 AP
   Coconut Shrimp...................85 AP
   Cornmeal-Crusted Salmon ......56 MC
   Coulibiac ....64 HF
   Crab Mousse ....32 AP
   Crab Tartlets.................... 122 AP

   Crab Tarts............................36 HF
   Crepes À La Crab ....26 BR
   Dilled Snapper Fry ....76 SF
   Fish And Rice Casserole ....80 CA
   Five-Spice Shrimp.................70 SF
   Hot Crab Dip.......................16 AP
   Island Fish Stir-Fry...............72 SF
   Just For The Halibut.............57 MC
   Lobster Chowder..................39 HF
   Lobster Newburg ....70 BR
   Marinated Shrimp .... 120 AP
   Orange And Dill Salmon ....54 MC
   Oriental Tuna Casserole........68 CA
   Pad Thai..............................98 SF
   Pea And Shrimp Frittata
      Muffins ....58 BR
   Pot Stickers .... 118 AP
   Quick Tuna Casserole ....66 CA
   Salmon 'Chanted Evening ....52 MC
   Salmon Canapés...................56 AP
   Salmon Pasta.......................72 CA
   Salmon Potato Scallop...........74 CA
   Salmon Rice Bake ....77 CA
   Sauced Crab Ball ....12 AP
   Scallop Attraction ....40 HF
   Scallops With Bacon ....63 AP
   Sea Bass À La Caesar ....56 MC
   Seafood Curry Dip................30 HF
   Seafood Delight...................82 CA
   Seafood Enchiladas...............84 CA
   Seafood In Black Bean Sauce ....84 SF
   Seafood Quiche....................42 BR
   Shrimp And Artichokes.........68 SF
   Shrimp And Asparagus
      Stir-Fry............................70 SF
   Shrimp And Pea Stir-Fry ....81 SF
   Shrimp And Pork Noodles......86 SF
   Shrimp Ball ....31 AP
   Shrimp Casserole.................81 CA
   Shrimp Chow Mein...............44 SF

MOST LOVED COOKBOOKS KEY: Appetizers **AP** • Brunches **BR** • Casseroles **CA** • Cookies **CO** • Festive Baking **FB** • Holiday Favourites **HF** • Main Courses **MC** • Salads & Dressings **SA** • Slow Cooker Creations **SC** • Stir-fries **SF** • Summertime Desserts **SD** • Treats **TR**

F

Shrimp Cocktail .... 115 AP	Fresh Fruit Betty ....71 TR	Mud Pie............................. 108 SD
Shrimp Cocktail ....38 HF	Fresh Fruit Salad ....78 SA	Peach Gelato .... 122 SD
Shrimp Creole ....77 SF	Fresh Herb Tea ....9 BR	Peach Melba Sundaes ....28 SD
Shrimp Ecstasy ....72 SF	Fresh Saskatoon Pie....................8 SD	Peachsicle Slice......................95 SD
Shrimp Fried Rice ....78 SF	Fried Rice	Piña Colada Pie .... 100 SD
Shrimp Mango Curry ....64 MC	Chicken ....78 SF	Raspberry Freeze .... 121 SD
Shrimp Salad Wraps ....82 AP	Chicken Vegetable..................64 SF	Strawberry Banana Frozen
Shrimp Spread ....30 AP	Shrimp ....78 SF	Yogurt .... 116 SD
Smoked Salmon Muffins ....24 BR	Special Ham ....94 SF	Strawberry Freeze................ 102 SD
Smothered Halibut ....78 CA	Fried Varenyky.........................82 HF	Sundae Dessert......................98 SD
Speedy Shrimp.......................85 SF	Frittatas	Swirl Ice Cream With Grilled
Surprise Company Dish...........69 CA	Chicken And Leek Frittata........59 BR	Cake And Berries ....48 SD
Surprise Spread ....6 AP	Pea And Shrimp Frittata	Tri-Colour Angel Roll ....92 SD
Sweet-And-Sour Shrimp ....80 SF	Muffins ....58 BR	Vanilla Coconut Ice Cream... 112 SD
Three Seafood Fry ....74 SF	Ribbon Zucchini Frittata.........60 BR	White Chocolate
Triple Seafood Noodles ....67 HF	Frosty Peanut Butter Pie .... 104 SD	Ice Cream .... 112 SD
Tuna Casserole ....70 CA	Frozen Banana Rockets............. 106 SD	White Chocolate
Veal Oscar ....16 MC	Frozen Cheesecake Bites .... 113 TR	Orange Chill......................87 SD
Fish & Seafood, see also Shrimp	Frozen Desserts	Frozen Fudge Pops.................. 109 SD
Fish And Fennel Parcels ....60 MC	Baked Alaska....................... 106 SD	Frozen Mocha Cheesecake........86 SD
Fish And Rice Casserole ....80 CA	Banana Split .... 110 SD	Fruit 'N' Nut Loaf, Festive ....96 FB
Five-Minute Fudge .... 108 HF	Cran-Raspberry Ice .... 116 SD	Fruit And Honey Bars ....56 FB
Five-Spice Shrimp........................70 SF	Creamy Ice Pops.................. 109 SD	Fruit And Nut Loaf ....98 FB
Flan, Cantaloupe ....12 SD	Drumstick Cake ....84 SD	Fruit Bark, Almond .... 107 HF
Flatbread With Spinach And	Frosty Peanut Butter Pie .... 104 SD	Fruit Betty, Fresh ....71 TR
Onions, Cornmeal ....92 AP	Frozen Banana Rockets......... 106 SD	Fruit Cobbler.............................26 FB
Florentine, Eggs...........................50 BR	Frozen Fudge Pops............... 109 SD	Fruit Cookies, Merry ....96 CO
Freezer Almond Cranberry Buns 110 FB	Frozen Mocha Cheesecake......86 SD	Fruit Crostini, Grilled Brie And......36 AP
Freezer Tomatoes.........................64 CA	Ginger Sorbet With Grilled	Fruit Dip
French Dressing .... 106 SA	Mangoes .... 118 SD	Caramel...............................19 AP
French Onion Soup ....14 SC	Ice Cream Cake ....88 SD	Cool ....35 SD
French Toast	Ice Cream Sandwiches ....96 SD	Easy ....19 AP
Baked Vanilla French Toast......36 BR	Ice Cream Toffee Slice............96 SD	Peanut Butter ....19 AP
Cinnamon Buns....................38 BR	Kiwifruit Sorbet.................... 120 SD	Yogurt ....34 SD
Fruit-Full French Toast ....36 BR	Layered Gelato Cake ....90 SD	Fruit Kabobs.............................34 SD
French Toast Cinnamon Buns ......38 BR	Lively Lime Pie.................... 101 SD	Fruit Kabobs, Marshmallow........32 SD
French Toast, Blueberry	Macadamia Tortoni .... 114 SD	Fruit Muffins, Spiced ....88 FB
Streusel................................14 HF	Mango Macadamia	Fruit Pancakes, Nutty ....29 BR
French Tourtière ....63 HF	Sandwich..........................94 SD	Fruit Pizza..................................6 SD
Fresh Broccoli Casserole ....76 HF	Mango Melon Sorbet........... 120 SD	Fruit Pizza................................62 TR

MOST LOVED COOKBOOKS KEY: Appetizers **AP** • Brunches **BR** • Casseroles **CA** • Cookies **CO** • Festive Baking **FB** • Holiday Favourites **HF**
Main Courses **MC** • Salads & Dressings **SA** • Slow Cooker Creations **SC** • Stir-fries **SF** • Summertime Desserts **SD** • Treats **TR**

F to G

Fruit Pudding, Steamed ....84 HF
Fruit Roll, Biscuit..........................12 HF
Fruit Salads
    Fresh.......................................78 SA
    Old-Fashioned Waldorf...........74 SA
    Pineapple Boat Salad..............72 SA
    Quick.......................................74 SA
    Rum...76 SA
    Spiced.....................................13 HF
    Spiced.....................................78 BR
    Summer ....78 SA
    Vanilla Bean............................24 SD
Fruit Scrolls...................................35 FB
Fruitcake Cookies .... 104 CO
Fruitcakes
    Dundee Cake............................9 FB
    Favourite Fruitcake ....8 FB
    Festive Fruitcake ....6 FB
    Rich Dark Fruitcake.............. 120 HF
Fruit-Full French Toast..................36 BR
Fruity Almond Ring ....18 BR
Fruity Beans And Sausage ....40 SC
Fruity Beef Curry ....10 SF
Fruity Butter Lettuce Salad ....36 SA
Fruity Salsa ....36 AP
Fruity Tortillas...............................20 SD
Fudge
    Choco-Peanut .... 108 TR
    Five-Minute .... 108 HF
    Sauce................................... 108 SD
    Truffles, White Chocolate ..... 112 HF
    White Creme .... 108 TR
Fudge Pops, Frozen..................... 109 SD
Fudgy Chocolate Mints .... 122 TR
Fudgy Macaroons ....80 TR
Full-Of-Beans Turkey Pot ....94 SC

G

Garlic Crust, Thai Pizza On A .... 104 MC
Garlic Dressings
    Chili.......................................62 SA
    Creamy................................. 108 SA
    Lemon....................................46 SA
Garlic Marinade............................70 MC
Garlic Meatballs, Honey ....46 MC
Garlic Sauce, Honey ....46 MC
Garlic-Stuffed Pork Roast.............68 MC
Gelato
    Mango ....90 SD
    Peach .... 122 SD
    Raspberry ....90 SD
Gelato Cake, Layered ....90 SD
Giant Candy Bar Cookies ....32 TR
Ginger Beef ....16 SF
Ginger Beef Stew ....56 SC
Ginger Beef, Saucy ....14 SF
Ginger Cookies, Carrot..................12 CO
Ginger Cookies, Rolled .... 114 CO
Ginger Crowns, Marmalade..........89 FB
Ginger Dressing .... 112 SA
Ginger Fig Cake, Sticky ....14 TR
Ginger Marinade...........................39 MC
Ginger Muffins, Batter-Ready ....8 HF
Ginger Scones ....92 FB
Ginger Sorbet.............................. 118 SD
Ginger Sorbet With
    Grilled Mangoes................. 118 SD
Gingerbread Cookies.................. 116 HF
Gingerbread Pull-Aparts .... 104 FB
Gingerbread Stars ....30 FB
Gingerbread, Pear Flower.............18 FB
Gingersnap Crumb Crust ....18 TR
Gingersnaps..................................62 CO
Glaze
    Apricot ....62 TR
    Coffee.....................................12 HF
    Coffee.....................................16 BR
    Coffee.....................................88 CO
    Easy ....46 TR
    Lemon.................................. 117 TR
    Lemon........................... 36, 40 CO
Glazed Coffee Balls.......................88 CO
Glazed Dill Carrots ....96 BR
Glazed Meatballs...........................37 HF
Glazed Meatballs, Maple-............72 AP
Glazed Parsnips ....68 HF
Glazed Wings .... 108 AP
Glazes, see Icings & Glazes
Glimmering Slice..........................61 TR
Golden Glazed Chicken............ 111 MC
Good Ol' Nuts 'N' Bolts ....26 HF
Goulash, Hungarian ....55 SC
Graham Cracker Coating ....92 CO
Graham Crumb Crust ..... 24, 60, 61 TR
Granola Banana Bread..................20 BR
Grape Salad, Spinach ....87 BR
Grasshopper Pie ....80 SD
Gravy
    Beefy Onion ....12 MC
    Chicken ....84 MC
    Herb.......................................68 MC
    Pot Roast ....46 SC
    Poultry...................................54 HF
Greek Bake, Creamy.....................10 CA
Greek Dressing ....12 SA
Greek Salad ....12 SA
Green Bean Stir-Fry .... 106 SF
Green Chili Snacks .... 119 AP
Green Goddess Dressing..............34 SA
Green Goddess Salad ....34 SA
Green Onion Cakes .... 116 AP
Green Onion Whirls ....34 HF
Green Salad With Grilled
    Peppers, Mixed ....43 SA
Greens Stir-Fry, Beef And ....22 SF
Greens, Chicken And....................40 SF
Greens, Lemon Pepper..................96 BR
Greens, Stir-Fried Honey .... 116 SF
Grilled Brie And Fruit Crostini....36 AP
Grilled Desserts
    Apple Cream Quesadillas.........22 SD

MOST LOVED COOKBOOKS KEY: Appetizers **AP** • Brunches **BR** • Casseroles **CA** • Cookies **CO** • Festive Baking **FB** • Holiday Favourites **HF**
Main Courses **MC** • Salads & Dressings **SA** • Slow Cooker Creations **SC** • Stir-fries **SF** • Summertime Desserts **SD** • Treats **TR**

G to H

Banana Quesadillas .... 22 SD
Fruit Kabobs .... 34 SD
Ginger Sorbet With Grilled
    Mangoes .... 118 SD
Grilled Peaches .... 33 SD
Grilled Pineapple Chunks .... 32 SD
Margaritagrill .... 30 SD
Marshmallow Fruit Kabobs ...... 32 SD
Swirl Ice Cream With Grilled
    Cake And Berries .... 48 SD
Grilled Mangoes .... 118 SD
Grilled Peaches .... 33 SD
Grilled Peppers, Mixed Green
    Salad With .... 43 SA
Grilled Pineapple Chunks .... 32 SD
Grilled Veggie Salad .... 42 SA
Grilling
    A Round Of Draft .... 10 MC
    Barbecued Beef Ribs .... 40 MC
    Beef Kabobs With Oregano
        And Onion .... 36 MC
    Best Pork Chops .... 70 MC
    Bulgogi .... 38 MC
    Buttered Steak And Shrimp ... 22 MC
    Butterflied Chicken .... 86 MC
    Cornmeal-Crusted Salmon .... 56 MC
    Fish And Fennel Parcels .... 60 MC
    Honey Ham Steaks .... 78 MC
    Lamb Chops .... 82 MC
    Orange And Dill Salmon .... 54 MC
    Peppercorn Roast .... 6 MC
    Rack of Lamb .... 82 MC
    Salmon 'Chanted Evening .... 52 MC
    Salsa-Stuffed Steak .... 28 MC
    Sea Bass À La Caesar .... 56 MC
    Spicy Stuffed Beef .... 14 MC
    Steak With Mushrooms
        And Onions .... 30 MC
    Steak With Spice Coating ..... 20 MC
    Sweet Heat Peanut

Chicken .... 92 MC
Ground Beef
    Company Meatloaf .... 43 MC
    Honey Garlic Meatballs .... 46 MC
    Mushroom-Stuffed
        Meatloaf .... 44 MC
    No-Fuss Stroganoff .... 49 MC
    Tourtière Québécoise .... 48 MC
Gumdrop Cookies .... 22 CO

Halibut, Just For The .... 57 MC
Halibut, Smothered .... 78 CA
Halloween Black Moons .... 122 CO
Ham
    Baked .... 75 BR
    Baked .... 78 MC
    Honey Ham Steaks .... 78 MC
    Redcurrant And
        Mustard-Glazed .... 50 HF
    Salmon Canapés .... 56 AP
    Slow Cooker Baked .... 114 SC
Ham And Cheese Ball .... 34 AP
Ham And Cheese Spread .... 34 AP
Ham And Pasta Bake .... 114 CA
Ham Casserole .... 116 CA
Ham Fried Rice, Special .... 94 SF
Ham Roll Canapés .... 34 AP
Ham Strata, Pepper And .... 18 HF
Ham Veggie Scallop .... 112 CA
Ham With Cranberry .... 78 MC
Ham, see Pork
Hamburger Pacific .... 8 CA
Handy Dandy Chicken .... 42 CA
Hash
    Chinese-Style .... 16 CA
    Corned Beef .... 64 BR
    Spiced Sweet Potato .... 94 BR
Hash Brown Potatoes, Spiced .... 92 BR
Hash Browns, Best .... 17 HF
Hash Browns, Oven .... 92 BR

Hazelnut Muffins, Mocha .... 86 FB
Hazelnut Sauce .... 92 MC
Hens, Cornish .... 118 MC
Herb Bread Ring .... 12 BR
Herb Gravy .... 68 MC
Herb Rub, Onion .... 14 MC
Herb Tea, Fresh .... 9 BR
Herb-Crusted Pork .... 66 MC
Herbed Barley Risotto .... 32 SC
Herbed Beef Tenderloin .... 8 MC
Herbed Rouladen, Broiled .... 24 MC
Hermits .... 50 TR
Hermits .... 8 CO
Hint O' Mint Squares .... 52 FB
Holiday Chicken .... 116 MC
Holiday Whirls .... 34 HF
Hollandaise Sauce, Jiffy .... 16 MC
Homemade Bread Crumbs .... 80 CA
Homemade Cocktail Sauce .... 13 AP
Honey Bars, Fruit And .... 56 FB
Honey Carrots, Cinnamon .... 76 HF
Honey Garlic Meatballs .... 46 MC
Honey Garlic Sauce .... 46 MC
Honey Greens, Stir-Fried .... 116 SF
Honey Ham Steaks .... 78 MC
Honey Jewel Cake .... 122 HF
Honey Lemon Icing .... 30 FB
Honey Mustard Butter .... 22 MC
Honey Mustard Dressing .... 116 SA
Honey Mustard Sauce .... 78 MC
Honey, Cinnamon .... 76 HF
Horseradish Dressing, Creamy ... 66 SA
Horseradish Sauce .... 6 MC
Horseradish Sauce, Creamy ..... 60 HF
Hot Buttered Cranberry .... 10 SC
Hot Chocolate, Caramel .... 6 SC
Hot Crab Dip .... 16 AP
Hot Cross Muffins .... 88 FB
Hot Mushroom Dip .... 40 AP
Hot Potato Salad, Italian .... 100 SA

MOST LOVED COOKBOOKS KEY: Appetizers **AP** • Brunches **BR** • Casseroles **CA** • Cookies **CO** • Festive Baking **FB** • Holiday Favourites **HF**
Main Courses **MC** • Salads & Dressings **SA** • Slow Cooker Creations **SC** • Stir-fries **SF** • Summertime Desserts **SD** • Treats **TR**

H to L

Hot Spiced Cranberry................10 SC
Hot Tamale Two-Step ....28 CA
Hot Tea Wassail..............................8 SC
Hungarian Goulash ....55 SC

I

Ice Cream
    Cake ....88 SD
    Peanut Butter Dip.....................19 AP
    Sandwiches ....96 SD
    Toffee Slice ....96 SD
    Treat, Peanut..............................64 TR
    Vanilla Coconut ....112 SD
    White Chocolate.....................112 SD
    With Grilled Cake And
        Berries, Swirl ....48 SD
Ice Pops, Creamy ....109 SD
Ice, Cran-Raspberry ....116 SD
Icebox Cookies, Lemon ....36 CO
Icebox Ribbons..............................40 TR
Icing
    Almond ....102 HF
    Caramel ....103 HF
    Chocolate ....14 CO
    Chocolate Coffee......................96 TR
    Chocolate Orange......................6 TR
    Orange..12 CO
    Royal ....116 CO
    Rum..44 TR
    Vanilla................................. 82, 88 TR
    White Chocolate........................16 TR
Icings & Glazes
    Almond Buttercream Icing ......16 FB
    Almond Glaze........................100 FB
    Basic Cookie Glaze ....38 FB
    Caramel Icing ....20 FB
    Choco Cream Cheese Icing.....62 FB
    Chocolate Glaze ....22 FB
    Honey Lemon Icing ....30 FB
    White Chocolate Glaze............13 FB
Impossible Quiche........................44 BR
Indian-Spiced Beef ....23 SF
Instant Glazed Parsnips ....68 HF
Irish Cream....................................22 HF
Island Fish Stir-Fry ....72 SF
Italian Dressing..........................104 SA
Italian Hot Potato Salad............100 SA

J

Jack-O'-Lantern Cookies ....118 CO
Jalapeño Cheese...........................24 AP
Jalapeño Jelly ....24 AP
Jam Jams ....42 CO
Jam Tarts ....74 FB
Jambalaya Casserole ....18 CA
Japanese Cabbage Salad ....52 SA
Japanese Shrimp Salad ....52 SA
Jazzy Jerk Soup ....26 SC
Jelly Salad, Cranberry ....68 SA
Jerk Soup, Jazzy ....26 SC
Jiffy Hollandaise Sauce................16 MC
Jiffy Mushroom Rolls ....98 AP
Juice, Champagne Orange............6 BR
Juicy Berries ....10 TR
Just For The Halibut....................57 MC

K

Kabobs
    Beef Kabobs With Oregano
        And Onion..........................36 MC
    Chili Lemon Shrimp ....64 AP
    Fruit..34 SD
    Marshmallow Fruit ....32 SD
    Polynesian Satay.......................94 AP
    Sesame Kabobs With
        Spinach ....39 MC
    Sesame Pork Balls ....89 AP
    Yakitori .... 110 AP
Kidney Bean Dip ....8 AP
King Artichoke Dip ....30 HF
Kisses, Lemon Meringue............84 CO
Kisses, Meringue ....84 CO
Kiwi With Orange Custard ....26 SD
Kiwifruit Sorbet ....120 SD
Knotty Cinnamon Buns ....106 FB
Kung Pao Chicken ....102 MC
Kung Pao Chicken ....62 SF
Kung Pao Sauce ....102 MC

L

Lamb
    Cassoulet ....118 CA
    Chops..82 MC
    Creole..116 CA
    Moroccan Lamb Stew ....122 SC
    Moussaka ....120 CA
    Rack Of.......................................82 MC
    Scotch Broth ....15 SC
    Shanks In Tomato
        Wine Sauce ....80 MC
    Shepherd's Pie........................122 CA
    Slow Cooker Dolmades ....34 SC
    Slow Cooker Lamb Curry .....118 SC
    Sun-Dried Tomato Lamb.......120 SC
Lamb Creole...............................116 CA
Lasagna ....14 CA
Lasagna ....68 SC
Lasagna
    Phyllo ....62 BR
    Polenta ....94 CA
    Vegetarian Pesto......................92 CA
Latté, Café....................................10 BR
Layered Camembert....................50 AP
Layered Cucumber Salad ....72 SA
Layered Gelato Cake ....90 SD
Layered Lemon............................70 SD
Layered Salad, Multi-...................20 SA
Layered Salad, Rio Ranchero ....22 SA
Layered Sausage Casserole......... 108 CA
Lazy Cabbage Roll Casserole ....19 CA
Lazy Daisy Cake............................8 TR
Lazy Perogy Casserole ....90 CA
Lebkuchen....................................44 FB
Leek Frittata, Chicken And ....59 BR

MOST LOVED COOKBOOKS KEY: Appetizers **AP** • Brunches **BR** • Casseroles **CA** • Cookies **CO** • Festive Baking **FB** • Holiday Favourites **HF**
Main Courses **MC** • Salads & Dressings **SA** • Slow Cooker Creations **SC** • Stir-fries **SF** • Summertime Desserts **SD** • Treats **TR**

L to M

Leftover Pasta Salad ....88 SA	Lime Dressing........................102 SA	Mango Gelato..........................90 SD
Lemon Bars ....84 TR	Lime Meringue Pie ....58 SD	Mango Macadamia
Lemon Chiffon ....52 SD	Lime Pear Salad ....46 HF	Sandwich............................94 SD
Lemon Coconut Angel ....39 SD	Lime Pie, Lively....................101 SD	Mango Melon Sorbet............120 SD
Lemon Cookies ....40 CO	Lime Poppy Seed Cake..........10 TR	Mango Raspberry Trifles.......56 TR
Lemon Cookies,	Liquid Gold Sauce ....35 BR	Mango Rum Fluff ....50 SD
Chocolate-Dipped ....36 CO	Little Dilled Snacks ....120 SA	Mango Sauce, Curried
Lemon Crackles......................74 CO	Lively Lime Pie....................101 SD	Pork And ....88 SF
Lemon Cranberry Couscous......102 BR	Loaves, see also Yeast Breads	Mango Smoothies......................8 BR
Lemon Crunch ....90 TR	Apple Loaf ....118 TR	Mango Torte...........................42 SD
Lemon Dill Dressing ....56 SA	Chocolate Banana Bread ....94 FB	Mangoes, Ginger Sorbet
Lemon Dressing, Creamy ....16 SA	Festive Fruit 'N' Nut Loaf.......96 FB	With Grilled ....118 SD
Lemon Dressing, Light ....26 SA	Fruit And Nut Loaf..............98 FB	Mangoes, Grilled..................118 SD
Lemon Filling ....84 CO	Lemon Loaf ....117 TR	Manhattan Clam Chowder ....18 SC
Lemon Filling ....90 TR	Orange Eggnog Loaf ....94 FB	Many Jewels Stir-Fry ....104 SF
Lemon Garlic Dressing ....46 SA	Loaves, see Breads & Loaves	Maple Orange Whipped
Lemon Glaze ....117 TR	Loaves, see Breads & Quick Breads	Cream ....98 HF
Lemon Glaze .... 36, 40 CO	Lobster Chowder....................39 HF	Maple Pears, Poached ....68 TR
Lemon Grass Pork ....76 MC	Lobster Newburg ....70 BR	Maple Pork Patties ....74 BR
Lemon Grass Pork Bowl...........102 SF	Lollipop Cookies.................114 CO	Maple Sauce ....72 AP
Lemon Icebox Cookies ....36 CO		Maple-Glazed Meatballs.........72 AP
Lemon Icing, Honey...............30 FB	Macadamia Mounds,	Margarita Pie, Strawberry......78 SD
Lemon Loaf ....117 TR	Cranberry ....112 CO	Margaritagrill..........................30 SD
Lemon Meringue Kisses.........84 CO	Macadamia Sandwich,	Margo's Rosemary Chicken........90 MC
Lemon Meringue Squares ....118 BR	Mango ....94 SD	Marinade, Vegetable..............51 SA
Lemon Mousse Pie ....54 SD	Macadamia Sundaes, Banana......66 TR	Marinades
Lemon Pepper Greens............96 BR	Macadamia Tortoni...............114 SD	Beer......................................10 MC
Lemon Pepper, Easy...............88 CA	Macaroni And Cheese ....86 CA	Garlic...................................70 MC
Lemon Pie, Upside-Down......56 SD	Macaroni Salad, Main ....86 SA	Ginger..................................39 MC
Lemon Shortbread Slices.........114 HF	Macaroni, Crunchy Vegetable......88 CA	Red Wine..............................36 MC
Lemon Shrimp, Chili ....64 AP	Macaroons ....22 CO	Marinated Feta.....................122 SA
Lemon Sponge Custard ....120 BR	Macaroons, Cherry Coconut ......28 TR	Marinated Onion Rings ......122 SA
Lemon Trifle, Blueberry ......122 BR	Macaroons, Fudgy ....80 TR	Marinated Shrimp ....120 AP
Lemon, Layered......................70 SD	Main Macaroni Salad ....86 SA	Marmalade Ginger Crowns.......89 FB
Lentil Potato Mash ....37 SC	Make-Ahead Eggs Benedict.......16 HF	Marmalade Orange Sauce.......88 MC
Lentil Rice Rolls..................104 SC	Make-Ahead Potatoes ....36 SC	Marmalade-Glazed
Lentil Soup, Squash And ......25 SC	Mandarin Beef ....37 SF	Sweet Potatoes...................74 HF
Lettuce Salad, Warm Bacon ......34 SA	Mandarin Chocolate Biscotti ......48 FB	Mars Bars Squares ....74 TR
Lettuce Wraps ....86 AP	Mandarin Poppy Seed Salad ......44 HF	Marshmallow Delights ....110 TR
Light Lemon Dressing ....26 SA	Mango Curry, Shrimp ....64 MC	Marshmallow Fruit Kabobs......32 SD

MOST LOVED COOKBOOKS KEY: Appetizers **AP** • Brunches **BR** • Casseroles **CA** • Cookies **CO** • Festive Baking **FB** • Holiday Favourites **HF**
Main Courses **MC** • Salads & Dressings **SA** • Slow Cooker Creations **SC** • Stir-fries **SF** • Summertime Desserts **SD** • Treats **TR**

M

Marshmallow Squares,
    Tropical .... 117 BR
Marshmallows, Chocolate .... 102 TR
Martini Dressing .... 108 SA
Marzipan Bars .... 102 HF
Mascarpone Sauce, Orange .... 32 SD
Mash, Lentil Potato .... 37 SC
Mashed Potato Salad .... 98 SA
Matrimonial Squares .... 86 TR
Mayonnaise
    Artichoke Dip .... 28 AP
    Corned Beef Mousse .... 30 AP
    Crab Mousse .... 32 AP
    Dilly Dip .... 17 AP
Mayonnaise Dressing, Simple .... 27 SA
Meat Canapés, Cheesy .... 58 AP
Meat Pie
    Tourtière Québécoise .... 48 MC
Meat Sauce .... 14 CA
Meatball Stew .... 70 SC
Meatball Stew, Porcupine .... 20 CA
Meatballs
    Crabapple .... 37 HF
    Cranberry .... 100 AP
    Glazed .... 37 HF
    Honey Garlic .... 46 MC
    Maple-Glazed .... 72 AP
    Polynesian .... 122 AP
    Sesame Pork Balls .... 89 AP
    Spanish .... 74 AP
    "Sweetish" .... 70 SC
    With Chutney Sauce .... 96 AP
Meatless Entrees
    Bean Sprouts And Peppers ... 120 SF
    Braised Vegetables .... 116 SF
    Cashew Vegetable Stir-Fry .... 110 SF
    Cheese Strata .... 102 CA
    Chili Black Beans .... 105 SC
    Chinese Stir-Fry
        Vegetables .... 106 SF

    Chop-Chop Teriyaki Tofu ..... 114 SF
    Crunchy Vegetable
        Macaroni .... 88 CA
    Diced Tofu And Noodles ...... 112 SF
    Easy Burritos .... 102 SC
    Eggplant Parmigiana .... 94 CA
    Eggplant Pasta Bake .... 96 CA
    Green Bean Stir-Fry .... 106 SF
    Lazy Perogy Casserole .... 90 CA
    Lentil Rice Rolls .... 104 SC
    Macaroni And Cheese .... 86 CA
    Many Jewels Stir-Fry .... 104 SF
    Pasta Primavera .... 108 SF
    Polenta Lasagna .... 94 CA
    Ratatouille .... 98 SC
    Rice Veggie Casserole .... 100 CA
    Sesame Snow Peas .... 120 SF
    Shanghai Noodles .... 122 SF
    Southwestern Casserole .... 100 CA
    Spicy Beans And Rice .... 102 SC
    Squash And Dumplings .... 98 SC
    Stir-Fried Honey Greens .... 116 SF
    Vegetable Couscous .... 118 SF
    Vegetable Curry .... 100 SC
    Vegetable Shepherd's Pie .... 98 CA
    Vegetarian Pesto
        Lasagna .... 92 CA
Meatloaf
    Company .... 43 MC
    Mushroom-Stuffed .... 44 MC
Mediterranean Chicken And
    Bean Casserole .... 44 CA
Melba Sauce .... 28 SD
Melon Banana Splits .... 28 SD
Melon Sorbet, Mango .... 120 SD
Meringue Crust .... 56 SD
Meringue Kisses .... 84 CO
Meringue Kisses, Lemon .... 84 CO
Meringue Pie, Lime .... 58 SD
Meringue Pie, Raspberry .... 60 SD

Meringue Shortcake,
    Strawberry .... 52 TR
Meringue Squares, Lemon .... 118 BR
Meringues, Coffee .... 82 CO
Meringues, Pineapple Coconut .... 43 SD
Merry Fruit Cookies .... 96 CO
Mexican Enchiladas .... 64 BR
Mexican Salad .... 32 SA
Mexican Snackies .... 54 AP
Midnight Mints .... 76 TR
Millionaire Squares .... 78 TR
Mince Tarts .... 72 FB
Mincemeat .... 94 HF
Mincemeat
    Fruit Scrolls .... 35 FB
    Mince Tarts .... 72 FB
    Mincemeat Bites .... 34 FB
    Mincemeat Nut Bread .... 97 FB
    Mincemeat Puffs .... 36 FB
    Mincemeat Squares .... 56 FB
Mincemeat Bites .... 34 FB
Mincemeat Nut Bread .... 97 FB
Mincemeat Pie .... 94 HF
Mincemeat Puffs .... 36 FB
Mincemeat Squares .... 56 FB
Mincemeat Tarts .... 95 HF
Mini Pumpkin Pies .... 98 HF
Mini-Cheesecakes, Berry .... 104 BR
Mini-Chip Cheesecakes .... 25 TR
Mint Dressing, Creamy .... 96 SA
Mint Loaf, Cranberry .... 118 HF
Mint Papaya Salsa .... 25 AP
Mint Salad, Potato .... 96 SA
Minted Pita Chips .... 121 SA
Mints
    After-Dinner .... 122 TR
    Fudgy Chocolate .... 122 TR
Mixed Green Salad With
    Grilled Peppers .... 43 SA
Mixed Greens, Papaya And .... 16 SA

MOST LOVED COOKBOOKS KEY: Appetizers **AP** • Brunches **BR** • Casseroles **CA** • Cookies **CO** • Festive Baking **FB** • Holiday Favourites **HF**
Main Courses **MC** • Salads & Dressings **SA** • Slow Cooker Creations **SC** • Stir-fries **SF** • Summertime Desserts **SD** • Treats **TR**

M to N

Recipe	Page	Book
Mocha Cheesecake, Frozen	86	SD
Mocha Chiffon Pie, Chocolate	82	SD
Mocha Diamonds	108	CO
Mocha Hazelnut Muffins	86	FB
Mocha Mousse	121	BR
Molasses Cookies, Thick	54	CO
Molasses Drops, Soft	49	TR
Mole, Chicken	93	MC
Moons, Halloween Black	122	CO
Moroccan Chicken	88	SC
Moroccan Lamb Stew	122	SC
Moussaka	120	CA
Mousse		
Chocolate	56	TR
Corned Beef	30	AP
Crab	32	AP
Cucumber	80	BR
Mocha	121	BR
Pie, Lemon	54	SD
Mozzarella Salad, Tomato	84	BR
Mud Monsters	122	CO
Mud Pie	108	SD
Muffins		
Apple Streusel	120	TR
Batter-Ready Ginger	8	HF
Butterscotch	116	TR
Chipper	116	TR
Chocolate And Pear	21	BR
Cranberry Sparkle	84	FB
Hot Cross	88	FB
Mocha Hazelnut	86	FB
Pea And Shrimp Frittata	58	BR
Raspberry Cream	6	HF
Rummy Eggnog	87	FB
Smoked Salmon	24	BR
Spiced Fruit	88	FB
Strawberry Rhubarb	22	BR
Mulled Wine	10	SC
Mulled Wine	22	HF
Mulled Wine, Cranberry	10	SC
Multi-Layered Salad	20	SA
Mum's Apple Pie	67	FB
Mushroom Chicken Sauce	90	SC
Mushroom Cream Sauce	112	CA
Mushroom Cups	66	AP
Mushroom Filling	66	AP
Mushroom Rolls	98	AP
Mushroom Salad, Spinach	26	SA
Mushroom Soup, Chinese	12	SC
Mushroom Tarts	106	AP
Mushroom Turnovers	66	AP
Mushrooms		
Blue Stuffed	35	HF
Favourite	114	AP
Hot Mushroom Dip	40	AP
Jiffy Mushroom Rolls	98	AP
Simple Stuffed	35	HF
Spring Rolls	88	AP
Mushrooms And Onions, Steak With	30	MC
Mushroom-Stuffed Meatloaf	44	MC
Mustard Butter, Honey	22	MC
Mustard Dressing	17	SA
Mustard Dressings		
Basil	61	SA
Creamy	50	SA
Honey	116	SA
Mustard Sauce, Honey	78	MC
Mustard-Glazed Ham, Redcurrant And	50	HF
Nanaimo Bars	72	TR
Nanaimo Bars, Chocolate Cherry	100	HF
Nanaimo Bars, Peppermint	100	HF
Neapolitan Squares	54	FB
Nests, Egg	62	CO
Niçoise Salad	10	SA
No-Bake Cookies		
Apricot Balls	92	CO
Boiled Chocolate Cookies	94	CO
Chocolate Peanut Drops	90	CO
Cream Cheese Balls	92	CO
Glazed Coffee Balls	88	CO
Noodle Power	86	CO
Peanut Butter Balls	94	CO
Peanut Butter Chip Balls	90	CO
Toffee Cookies	86	CO
No-Fuss Stroganoff	49	MC
No-Fuss Stuffing	84	MC
Noodle Baskets	24	SF
Noodle Power	41	TR
Noodle Power	86	CO
Noodles & Pasta		
Black Bean Shrimp Noodles	82	SF
Chap Jae	34	SF
Curried Pork And Mango Sauce	88	SF
Diced Tofu And Noodles	112	SF
Lemon Grass Pork Bowl	102	SF
Noodle Baskets	24	SF
Pad Thai	98	SF
Pan-Fried Noodles	22	SF
Pasta Primavera	108	SF
Saucy Asian Dinner	96	SF
Shanghai Noodles	122	SF
Shrimp And Pork Noodles	86	SF
Thai Noodles	18	SF
Noodles, see Pasta & Noodles		
Noodles, Triple Seafood	67	HF
Nut Bread, Mincemeat	97	FB
Nut Loaf, Festive Fruit 'N'	96	FB
Nut Loaf, Fruit And	98	FB
Nut Pudding, Caramel	82	FB
Nut Rolls, Sour Cream	50	CO
Nutri-Cookies	48	TR
Nuts		
Candied	24	HF
Caramelized	112	AP

MOST LOVED COOKBOOKS KEY: Appetizers **AP** • Brunches **BR** • Casseroles **CA** • Cookies **CO** • Festive Baking **FB** • Holiday Favourites **HF** • Main Courses **MC** • Salads & Dressings **SA** • Slow Cooker Creations **SC** • Stir-fries **SF** • Summertime Desserts **SD** • Treats **TR**

N to P

Chocolate .... 102 TR
Roasted Pecans .... 117 SA
Sesame Walnut Topping ...... 118 SA
Spiced .... 118 SA
Sugar-Coated .... 112 AP
Nuts 'N' Bolts, Good Ol' .... 26 HF
Nutty Biscotti .... 67 CO
Nutty Biscotti,
   Chocolate-Dipped .... 67 CO
Nutty Cherry Shortbread .... 99 CO
Nutty Fruit Pancakes .... 29 BR
Nutty Shortbread Crust .... 64 SD

Oatmeal
   Best Drop Cookies .... 6 CO
   Boiled Chocolate Cookies ...... 94 CO
   Carrot Cookies .... 12 CO
   Carrot Ginger Cookies .... 12 CO
   Chocolate Peanut Drops .... 90 CO
   Crackerjack Cookies .... 76 CO
   Gumdrop Cookies .... 22 CO
   Spicy Dads .... 11 CO
Oatmeal Chip Cookies .... 37 TR
Oatmeal Chip Pizza .... 37 TR
Oatmeal Raisin Cookies .... 18 CO
Old-Fashioned Coffee Cake ..... 110 BR
Old-Fashioned Toffee .... 108 HF
Old-Fashioned Waldorf .... 74 SA
Omelette, Asparagus .... 54 BR
Omelette, Spinach And
   Bacon .... 56 BR
One-Dish Meal .... 12 CA
Onion Bake, Carrot .... 38 SC
Onion Beef Ragout .... 59 SC
Onion Butter .... 82 HF
Onion Butter, Varenyky With ..... 82 HF
Onion Cakes, Green .... 116 AP
Onion Gravy, Beefy .... 12 MC
Onion Herb Rub .... 14 MC
Onion Rings, Marinated .... 122 SA

Onion Soup, French .... 14 SC
Onion, Beef Kabobs With
   Oregano And .... 36 MC
Onions, Cornmeal Flatbread
   With Spinach And .... 92 AP
Onions, Steak With
   Mushrooms And .... 30 MC
Orange Almond Salad .... 39 SA
Orange And Dill Salmon .... 54 MC
Orange Beef And Broccoli .... 24 SF
Orange Blossom Bowls .... 122 SD
Orange Cake, Chocolate .... 6 TR
Orange Chicken .... 87 SC
Orange Chicken, Sweet .... 42 SF
Orange Chiffon Cake .... 40 SD
Orange Chiffon Pie .... 83 SD
Orange Chill, White Chocolate ... 87 SD
Orange Chocolate Cake .... 12 FB
Orange Chocolate Squares ...... 104 HF
Orange Cookies .... 109 HF
Orange Cranberry Wedges .... 91 FB
Orange Custard .... 26 SD
Orange Custard, Kiwi With .... 26 SD
Orange Custard,
   Strawberries With .... 26 SD
Orange Date Bars .... 116 BR
Orange Dressing .... 36 SA
Orange Dressing, Tangy .... 114 SA
Orange Eggnog Loaf .... 94 FB
Orange Icing .... 12 CO
Orange Icing, Chocolate .... 6 TR
Orange Juice, Champagne .... 6 BR
Orange Mascarpone Sauce .... 32 SD
Orange Poppy Seed Coleslaw ... 86 BR
Orange Poppy Seed Dressing ... 44 HF
Orange Poppy Seed Dressing ... 86 BR
Orange Pork .... 72 MC
Orange Salad, Radish And .... 64 SA
Orange Sauce .... 106 SC
Orange Sauce, Marmalade .... 88 MC

Orange Sauce, Pork With .... 106 SC
Orange Soufflé Clouds .... 59 SD
Orange Spritz .... 83 CO
Orange Swirls .... 44 SD
Orange Whipped Cream,
   Maple .... 98 HF
Orange, Yogurt And Poppy Seed
   Cheesecake .... 74 SD
Orange-Sauced Beets .... 78 HF
Oregano And Onion, Beef
   Kabobs With .... 36 MC
Oriental Cheese Spread .... 18 AP
Oriental Chicken Salad .... 52 SA
Oriental Rice Casserole .... 60 CA
Oriental Tuna Casserole .... 68 CA
Oriental Wings .... 108 AP
Ornaments, Cookie .... 114 CO
Oscar, Beef .... 16 MC
Oscar, Veal .... 16 MC
Oven Beef Roast .... 12 MC
Oven Cordon Bleu .... 6 MC
Oven Hash Browns .... 92 BR
Oven Scrambled Eggs .... 52 BR
Oven Stew .... 32 CA
Oven Tortilla Chips .... 10 AP
Overnight Coleslaw .... 54 SA

Pad Thai .... 98 SF
Pan Cordon Bleu .... 96 MC
Pancakes
   Apple Raisin .... 28 BR
   Blueberry Cream .... 30 BR
   Buttermilk .... 28 BR
   Nutty Fruit .... 29 BR
Panettone .... 116 FB
Pan-Fried Noodles .... 22 SF
Papaya And Mixed Greens .... 16 SA
Papaya Coconut Salsa .... 20 MC
Papaya Salsa, Mint .... 25 AP
Parfait Crab Salad .... 18 SA

MOST LOVED COOKBOOKS KEY: Appetizers **AP** • Brunches **BR** • Casseroles **CA** • Cookies **CO** • Festive Baking **FB** • Holiday Favourites **HF**
Main Courses **MC** • Salads & Dressings **SA** • Slow Cooker Creations **SC** • Stir-fries **SF** • Summertime Desserts **SD** • Treats **TR**

P

Parmesan Chicken Drumettes ......80 SC	Pasta Salads	Easy Peanut Butter Cookies .....58 CO
Parmesan Chicken Wings............80 AP	Leftover ....88 SA	Noodle Power ....86 CO
Parmesan Wings, Crusty...............80 AP	Main Macaroni ....86 SA	PBJ Crisps ....32 CO
Parmesan, Chicken ....89 MC	Pesto ....80 SA	Peanut Blossoms....................56 CO
Parmigiana, Chicken ....84 SC	Shrimp ....86 SA	Pie, Frosty............................ 104 SD
Parmigiana, Eggplant ....94 CA	Spinach ....82 SA	Peanut Butter Balls ....94 CO
Parsley Basil Pesto........................92 CA	Stuffed Tomato ....84 SA	Peanut Butter Chicken ....82 SC
Parsley Pesto Dressing ....82 SA	Pasta, see Noodles & Pasta	Peanut Butter Chip Balls.............90 CO
Parsley Sauce, Egg And ....66 HF	Pastry, also see Pies and Pastries	Peanut Butter Dip........................19 AP
Parsley Vinaigrette.......................10 SA	Pastries	Peanut Butter Hide-Aways..........36 TR
Parsnips, Glazed ....68 HF	Beef In ....18 MC	Peanut Chicken, Sweet Heat ......92 MC
Parsnips, Instant Glazed ....68 HF	Brie In ....35 AP	Peanut Dressing ....90 SA
Party Eggnog ....24 HF	Cream Cheese .... 66, 97 AP	Peanut Drops, Chocolate ....90 CO
Pasta & Noodles	Cream Cheese Danish .... 102 FB	Peanut Ice Cream Treat...............64 TR
Cacciatore Casserole................58 CA	Danish................. 102 FB	Peanut Pork Wraps......................90 SF
Chicken Noodles Romanoff.....56 CA	Processor Pecan....................70 FB	Peanut Rice Noodle Salad ....90 SA
Chicken Tetrazzini ....54 CA	Shortcrust..............................67 FB	Pear Flower Gingerbread.............18 FB
Creamed Turkey Noodle ....62 CA	Triangles With Pears ....75 FB	Pear Muffins, Chocolate And........21 BR
Creamy Greek Bake ....10 CA	Patties, Maple Pork.....................74 BR	Pear Salad, Lime..........................46 HF
Crunchy Vegetable	Pavlova.......................................36 SD	Pear Stir-Fry, Chili, Pork And ......93 SF
Macaroni ....88 CA	PBJ Crisps ....32 CO	Pears
Eggplant Pasta Bake ....96 CA	Pea And Shrimp	Caramelized ....75 FB
Ham And Pasta Bake .... 114 CA	Frittata Muffins ....58 BR	Pastry Triangles With ....75 FB
Hamburger Pacific ....8 CA	Pea Salad, Bacon And ....48 SA	Poached Maple ....68 TR
Lasagna ....14 CA	Pea Salad, Cheesy ....50 SA	Pecan Balls .... 110 HF
Lazy Perogy Casserole ....90 CA	Pea Soup, Split ....29 SC	Pecan Balls ....76 CO
Macaroni And Cheese ....86 CA	Pea Stir-Fry, Shrimp And ....81 SF	Pecan Bread, Cranberry............. 114 FB
One-Dish Meal ....12 CA	Peach Gelato .... 122 SD	Pecan Butter Cookies, Cherry.......26 CO
Oriental Tuna Casserole...........68 CA	Peach Melba Sundaes ....28 SD	Pecan Cakes, Fig And...................19 FB
Riviera Chicken Casserole ....52 CA	Peaches And Cream ....64 SD	Pecan Caramel Kisses ....31 TR
Salmon Pasta...........................72 CA	Peaches And Cream ....78 BR	Pecan Crust............................. 102 SD
Teener's Dish...........................11 CA	Peaches In Raspberry Sauce,	Pecan Pastry, Processor ....70 FB
Tuna Casserole ....70 CA	Poached ....22 SD	Pecan Salad, Strawberry..............14 SA
Vegetarian Pesto Lasagna ....92 CA	Peaches, Brandied ....70 TR	Pecans, Roasted...................... 117 SA
Wiener Pasta Bake .... 106 CA	Peaches, Grilled..........................33 SD	Pepper And Ham Strata ....18 HF
Zesty Beef Casserole ....6 CA	Peachsicle Slice...........................95 SD	Pepper Bread, Crisp Almond........34 HF
Pasta e Fagioli ....24 SC	Peachy Rhubarb Cobbler.............10 SD	Pepper Greens, Lemon................96 BR
Pasta Primavera .... 108 SF	Peanut Blossoms ....56 CO	Pepper Sauce, Roasted ....72 BR
Pasta Salad, Antipasto ....90 BR	Peanut Butter	Pepper Steak, Chinese.................52 SC
Pasta Salad, Dill ....90 BR	Chocolate Peanut Drops ....90 CO	Pepper Stir-Fry, Three..................32 SF

MOST LOVED COOKBOOKS KEY: Appetizers **AP** • Brunches **BR** • Casseroles **CA** • Cookies **CO** • Festive Baking **FB** • Holiday Favourites **HF**
Main Courses **MC** • Salads & Dressings **SA** • Slow Cooker Creations **SC** • Stir-fries **SF** • Summertime Desserts **SD** • Treats **TR**

P

Pepper, Easy Lemon .... 88 CA
Peppercorn Roast .... 6 MC
Peppered Chicken .... 60 SF
Peppermint Nanaimo Bars .... 100 HF
Peppers, Bean Sprouts And .... 120 SF
Peppers, Corn And
    Bean-Stuffed .... 92 SC
Perfect Cucumber Salad .... 72 SA
Perogies, see Varenyky
Perogy Casserole, Lazy .... 90 CA
Pesto Croutons, Basil .... 120 SA
Pesto Croutons, Tomato .... 120 SA
Pesto Dressing .... 80 SA
Pesto Dressing, Parsley .... 82 SA
Pesto Lasagna, Vegetarian .... 92 CA
Pesto Pasta Salad .... 80 SA
Pesto, Parsley Basil .... 92 CA
Phyllo Crust, Apples In A .... 76 FB
Phyllo Lasagna .... 62 BR
Phyllo Pastry,
    Beef Sprout Rolls .... 68 AP
Picadillo Pie ....26 CA
Pies
    Apples In A Phyllo Crust .... 76 FB
    Banana Cream Pie .... 63 SD
    Blueberry Pie .... 9 SD
    Captain's .... 76 CA
    Caramel Brownie Tart .... 70 FB
    Chicken Pot .... 48 CA
    Chicken Pot .... 66 BR
    Chocolate Mocha
        Chiffon Pie .... 82 SD
    Coconut Cream Pie .... 79 SD
    Corny Shepherd's .... 116 SC
    Cranberry Pie .... 64 FB
    Crustless Chicken .... 46 CA
    Easy Shepherd's .... 25 CA
    Fresh Saskatoon Pie .... 8 SD
    Frosty Peanut Butter Pie .... 104 SD
    Grasshopper Pie .... 80 SD

Lamb Shepherd's .... 122 CA
Lemon Mousse Pie .... 54 SD
Lime Meringue Pie .... 58 SD
Lively Lime Pie .... 101 SD
Mud Pie .... 108 SD
Mum's Apple Pie .... 67 FB
Orange Chiffon Pie .... 83 SD
Picadillo .... 26 CA
Piña Colada Pie .... 100 SD
Pineapple Glory Pie .... 62 SD
Pineapple Wink Pie .... 75 SD
Pink Velvet Pie .... 78 SD
Plum And Almond Tart .... 68 FB
Raspberry Meringue Pie .... 60 SD
Spinach Cheese .... 46 BR
Strawberry Freeze .... 102 SD
Strawberry Margarita Pie .... 78 SD
Strawberry Rhubarb Pie .... 8 SD
Tomato Basil .... 44 BR
Upside-Down Lemon Pie .... 56 SD
Vegetable Shepherd's .... 98 CA
Walnut Raisin Tart .... 66 FB
White Chocolate Orange
    Chill .... 87 SD
Pies & Pastries, Savoury
    Coulibiac .... 64 HF
    Crab Tarts .... 36 HF
    Cream Cheese Pastry .... 36 HF
    French Tourtière .... 63 HF
    Turkey Pies .... 48 HF
Pies & Pastries, Sweet
    Biscuit Fruit Roll .... 12 HF
    Butter Tarts .... 99 HF
    Christmas Cranapple Pies .... 96 HF
    Mincemeat Pie .... 94 HF
    Mincemeat Tarts .... 95 HF
    Mini Pumpkin Pies .... 98 HF
    Pilaf, Barley And Rice .... 71 HF
    Pilaf, Sweet Saffron .... 100 BR
    Piña Colada Cake .... 108 BR

Piña Colada Pie .... 100 SD
Pineapple And Coconut
    Chicken .... 100 MC
Pineapple Beef Stir-Fry .... 20 SF
Pineapple Boat Salad .... 72 SA
Pineapple Chiffon Cake .... 112 BR
Pineapple Chunks, Broiled .... 32 SD
Pineapple Chunks, Grilled .... 32 SD
Pineapple Citrus Punch .... 8 BR
Pineapple Coconut
    Meringues .... 43 SD
Pineapple Delight .... 72 SD
Pineapple Glory Pie .... 62 SD
Pineapple Salad, Tomato .... 62 SA
Pineapple Wink Pie .... 75 SD
Pink Dressing .... 111 SA
Pink Lady .... 69 SD
Pink Velvet Pie .... 78 SD
Pinwheels .... 106 TR
Pinwheels
    Chocolate .... 34 CO
    Cinnamon Roll Cookies .... 38 CO
    Date .... 34 CO
    Raspberry .... 34 CO
    Shortbread .... 28 CO
Pistachio Dessert .... 64 SD
Pistachio Salad .... 75 SA
Pita Chips, Minted .... 121 SA
Pizza
    Chipper .... 16 CO
    Cookie .... 36 TR
    Fruit .... 6 SD
    Fruit .... 62 TR
    Oatmeal Chip .... 37 TR
    Rainbow Chip .... 38 TR
Pizza Crust, Sugary .... 6 SD
Pizza On A Garlic Crust, Thai .... 104 MC
Plum And Almond Tart .... 68 FB
Plum Sauce .... 116 MC
Poached Maple Pears .... 68 TR

MOST LOVED COOKBOOKS KEY: Appetizers **AP** • Brunches **BR** • Casseroles **CA** • Cookies **CO** • Festive Baking **FB** • Holiday Favourites **HF** • Main Courses **MC** • Salads & Dressings **SA** • Slow Cooker Creations **SC** • Stir-fries **SF** • Summertime Desserts **SD** • Treats **TR**

P

Poached Peaches In Raspberry
    Sauce .... 22 SD
Polenta Lasagna .... 94 CA
Polynesian Meatballs .... 122 AP
Polynesian Ribs .... 74 MC
Polynesian Satay .... 94 AP
Popcorn
    White Chocolate .... 110 TR
    Caramel .... 60 AP
    Special Caramel .... 60 AP
Poppy Seed Cake, Lime .... 10 TR
Poppy Seed Cheesecake
    Orange, Yogurt And .... 74 SD
Poppy Seed Coleslaw, Orange .... 86 BR
Poppy Seed Dressing .... 110 SA
Poppy Seed Dressing .... 87 BR
Poppy Seed Dressing, Orange .... 44 HF
Poppy Seed Dressing, Orange .... 86 BR
Poppy Seed Loaf .... 20 BR
Poppy Seed Salad, Mandarin ..... 44 HF
Pops, Creamy Ice .... 109 SD
Pops, Frozen Fudge .... 109 SD
Porcupine Meatball Stew .... 20 CA
Pork
    Apricot Pork Loin Roast .... 58 HF
    Bacon Varenyky .... 82 HF
    Baked Ham .... 75 BR
    Baked Ham .... 78 MC
    Barbecue Shredded
        Pork Sandwiches .... 108 SC
    Barbecued Flavoured
        Pork Chops .... 70 MC
    Barbecued Flavoured Ribs .... 70 MC
    Barbecued Ribs .... 74 MC
    Best Pork Chops .... 70 MC
    Blue Cheesecake .... 44 AP
    Breakfast Strata .... 40 BR
    Brunch Dish .... 47 BR
    Cabbage Rolls .... 80 HF
    Cajun Chicken .... 76 SC

Cassoulet .... 118 CA
Celery-Sauced Chops .... 110 SC
Cheesy Meat Canapés .... 58 AP
Cherry Pork Chops .... 109 SC
Chicken Cordon Bleu .... 96 MC
Chili, Pork And
    Pear Stir-Fry .... 93 SF
Chinese Mushroom Soup .... 12 SC
Chunky Zucchini Soup .... 20 SC
Corny Shepherd's Pie .... 116 SC
Curried Pork And
    Mango Sauce .... 88 SF
Dumpling Casserole .... 50 CA
Easiest Ribs .... 112 SC
Easy Eggs Benny .... 50 BR
French Tourtière .... 63 HF
Fruity Beans And Sausage .... 40 SC
Garlic-Stuffed Pork Roast .... 68 MC
Ham And Cheese Ball .... 34 AP
Ham And Cheese Spread .... 34 AP
Ham And Pasta Bake .... 114 CA
Ham Casserole .... 116 CA
Ham Roll Canapés .... 34 AP
Ham Veggie Scallop .... 112 CA
Ham With Cranberry .... 78 MC
Herb-Crusted .... 66 MC
Honey Ham Steaks .... 78 MC
Impossible Quiche .... 44 BR
Jazzy Jerk Soup .... 26 SC
Jiffy Mushroom Rolls .... 98 AP
King Artichoke Dip .... 30 HF
Layered Sausage Casserole ... 108 CA
Lemon Grass .... 76 MC
Lemon Grass Pork Bowl .... 102 SF
Make-Ahead
    Eggs Benedict .... 16 HF
Maple Pork Patties .... 74 BR
Orange .... 72 MC
Oven Cordon Bleu .... 96 MC
Pad Thai .... 98 SF

Pan Cordon Bleu .... 96 MC
Peanut Pork Wraps .... 90 SF
Pepper And Ham Strata .... 18 HF
Polynesian Ribs .... 74 MC
Pork And Rice Dish .... 103 CA
Pork Chops Normandy .... 110 SC
Pork With Orange Sauce .... 106 SC
Pot Stickers .... 118 AP
Redcurrant And Mustard-
    Glazed Ham .... 50 HF
Ribbon Zucchini Frittata .... 60 BR
Salmon Canapés .... 56 AP
Saucy Asian Dinner .... 96 SF
Sausage And Potato Stew ...... 115 SC
Sausage Strata .... 110 CA
Sausage Stuffing .... 55 HF
Sausage Stuffing .... 84 MC
Sausage Stuffing Casserole ...... 55 HF
Scallops With Bacon .... 63 AP
Scrambled Breakfast .... 52 BR
Sesame Pork Balls .... 89 AP
Sesame Pork Stir-Fry .... 92 SF
Shrimp And Pork Noodles .... 86 SF
Slow Cooker Baked Ham .... 114 SC
Souper Supper .... 113 CA
Special Ham Fried Rice .... 94 SF
Spicy Sausage And Bread
    Stuffing .... 44 SC
Spinach And Bacon
    Omelette .... 56 BR
Spinach Dip #1 .... 26 AP
Split Pea Soup .... 29 SC
Stilton Puffs .... 32 HF
Stuffed Pork Loin .... 76 BR
Stuffed Turkey Scaloppine .... 120 MC
Sweet And Spicy
    Pork Casserole .... 104 CA
Sweet Bean Pot .... 40 SC
Sweet-And-Sour Pork .... 100 SF
Sweet-And-Sour Ribs .... 112 SC

MOST LOVED COOKBOOKS KEY: Appetizers **AP** • Brunches **BR** • Casseroles **CA** • Cookies **CO** • Festive Baking **FB** • Holiday Favourites **HF**
Main Courses **MC** • Salads & Dressings **SA** • Slow Cooker Creations **SC** • Stir-fries **SF** • Summertime Desserts **SD** • Treats **TR**

P to R

Recipe	Page	Book
Tournados	28	MC
Tourtière Québécoise	48	MC
Uptown Asparagus Chicken	66	BR
Wiener Pasta Bake	106	CA
Wieners And Beans	106	CA
Pork And Rice Dish	103	CA
Pork Chops Normandy	110	SC
Pork With Orange Sauce	106	SC
Pot Pie, Chicken	48	CA
Pot Pie, Chicken	66	BR
Pot Roast	46	SC
Pot Roast Gravy	46	SC
Pot Stickers	118	AP
Potato Cakes, Veggie	94	BR
Potato Mash, Lentil	37	SC
Potato Mint Salad	96	SA
Potato Salad	88	BR
Potato Salad	98	SA
Potato Salads		
Italian Hot	100	SA
Mashed	98	SA
Sweet	94	SA
Potato Skins, Snackin'	61	AP
Potato Stew, Sausage And	115	SC
Potatoes		
Autumn Bake	34	CA
Best Hash Browns	17	HF
Brunch Dish	47	BR
Captain's Pie	76	CA
Chicken Pot Pie	48	CA
Chicken Pot Pie	66	BR
Corned Beef Hash	64	BR
Crustless Chicken Pie	46	CA
Dressed Red	36	SC
Easy Shepherd's Pie	25	CA
Festive Scalloped Potatoes	70	HF
Ham Veggie Scallop	112	CA
Lamb Shepherd's Pie	122	CA
Layered Sausage Casserole	108	CA
Lazy Perogy Casserole	90	CA
Make-Ahead	36	SC
Oven Hash Browns	92	BR
Oven Stew	32	CA
Picadillo Pie	26	CA
Porcupine Meatball Stew	20	CA
Potato Salad	88	BR
Potatoes Extraordinaire	68	HF
Salmon Potato Scallop	74	CA
Seafood Delight	82	CA
Shipwreck	29	CA
Spiced Hash Brown Potatoes	92	BR
Squash Stew	32	CA
Sweet And Spicy Pork Casserole	104	CA
Swiss Steak Casserole	30	CA
Tater-Topped Beef Bake	24	CA
Vegetable Medley	98	BR
Vegetable Shepherd's Pie	98	CA
Veggie Potato Cakes	94	BR
Poultry Gravy	54	HF
Pound Cake, White Chocolate	16	TR
Primavera, Pasta	108	SF
Processor Pecan Pastry	70	FB
Pudding Brownies	116	BR
Puddings		
Apple Croissant	83	FB
Bread	82	FB
Caramel Nut	82	FB
Chocolate Eggnog	78	FB
Corn	97	BR
Croissant Strawberry	114	BR
Queen Of	82	FB
Raisin Bread	86	HF
Steamed Fruit	84	HF
Sticky Date	80	FB
Yorkshire	62	HF
Pull-Aparts, Breakfast	9	HF
Pull-Aparts, Gingerbread	104	FB
Pulled Tex Turkey	94	SC
Pumpkin Cheesecake	18	TR
Pumpkin Cookies	10	CO
Pumpkin Pies, Mini	98	HF
Punch		
Christmas	20	HF
Pineapple Citrus	8	BR
Sparkling Raspberry	6	BR

Q

Recipe	Page	Book
Queen Of Puddings	82	FB
Quesadilla Starters	111	AP
Quesadillas, Apple Cream	22	SD
Quesadillas, Banana	22	SD
Quiches		
Brunch Dish	47	BR
Chicken Veggie Crustless Quiche	42	BR
Impossible Quiche	44	BR
Seafood Quiche	42	BR
Spinach Cheese Pie	46	BR
Tomato Basil Pie	44	BR
Quick Fruit Salad	74	SA
Quick Salsa	48	AP
Quick Tuna Casserole	66	CA

R

Recipe	Page	Book
Rack Of Lamb	82	MC
Radish And Orange Salad	64	SA
Ragout, Onion Beef	59	SC
Rainbow Chip Cookies	38	TR
Rainbow Chip Pizza	38	TR
Raisin 'N' Bread Stuffing	14	MC
Raisin Braid, Swirled	113	FB
Raisin Bread Pudding	86	HF
Raisin Cake, Boiled	20	FB
Raisin Cobbler	28	FB
Raisin Cream Topping	38	BR
Raisin Filling	48, 118	CO
Raisin Filling	66	FB
Raisin Pancakes, Apple	28	BR
Raisin Sandwich Cookies	118	CO

MOST LOVED COOKBOOKS KEY: Appetizers **AP** • Brunches **BR** • Casseroles **CA** • Cookies **CO** • Festive Baking **FB** • Holiday Favourites **HF** • Main Courses **MC** • Salads & Dressings **SA** • Slow Cooker Creations **SC** • Stir-fries **SF** • Summertime Desserts **SD** • Treats **TR**

R

Raisin Sauce ....50 HF	Red Wine Sauce ....15 MC	Ribs
Raisin Tart, Walnut ....66 FB	Red Wine, Beef In.........................58 SC	Barbecue Beef........................46 SC
Raisin-Filled Cookies ....48 CO	Redcurrant And Mustard-	Barbecued ....74 MC
Raisins	Glazed Ham ....50 HF	Barbecued Beef ....40 MC
Carrot Cookies........................12 CO	Redcurrant Dressing.....................82 BR	Barbecued Flavoured..............70 MC
Carrot Ginger Cookies............12 CO	Refried Bean Dip ....52 AP	Easiest.................................. 112 SC
Chewy Cookie Clusters......... 103 CO	Refrigerator Cookies	Polynesian ....74 MC
Fruitcake Cookies.................. 104 CO	Butterscotch Cookies...............30 CO	Short ....42 MC
Hermits...................................... 8 CO	Checkerboard Shortbread ....28 CO	Sweet-And-Sour .... 112 SC
Jack-O'-Lantern Cookies .... 118 CO	Cherry Almond Butter	Rice
Merry Fruit Cookies ....96 CO	Cookies................................26 CO	Almond Chicken......................58 SF
Oatmeal Raisin Cookies ....18 CO	Cherry Pecan Butter Cookies ...26 CO	Arroz Con Pollo ....40 CA
Pumpkin Cookies....................10 CO	Chocolate Pinwheels ....34 CO	Bibimbap................................12 SF
Ranch Dressing, Spicy ....64 SA	Chocolate-Dipped Lemon	Chicken 'N' Rice ....42 CA
Raspberry Bars..............................58 FB	Cookies................................36 CO	Chicken Divan ....39 CA
Raspberry Cheesecake,	Cinnamon Roll Cookies ....38 CO	Chicken Fried Rice ....78 SF
Almond And...........................72 SD	Cloverleaf Shortbread...............28 CO	Chicken Vegetable
Raspberry Cheesecake,	Cream Cheese Cookies.............30 CO	Fried Rice............................64 SF
Chocolate ....76 SD	Cream Cheese Crescents..........31 CO	Chinese-Style Hash ....16 CA
Raspberry Chicken........................84 SC	Date Pinwheels........................34 CO	Dolmades................................62 AP
Raspberry Cream Muffins................6 HF	Lemon Icebox Cookies ....36 CO	Fish And Rice Casserole ....80 CA
Raspberry Dessert.........................60 TR	Merry Fruit Cookies ....96 CO	Handy Dandy Chicken ....42 CA
Raspberry Dressing..................... 114 SA	Nutty Cherry Shortbread.........99 CO	Jambalaya Casserole ....18 CA
Raspberry Freeze .... 121 SD	PBJ Crisps................................32 CO	Lazy Cabbage
Raspberry Gelato..........................90 SD	Raspberry Pinwheels................34 CO	Roll Casserole......................19 CA
Raspberry Ice, Cran- .... 116 SD	Shortbread ....98 CO	Oriental Rice Casserole ....60 CA
Raspberry Meringue Pie ....60 SD	Shortbread Pinwheels..............28 CO	Porcupine Meatball Stew.........20 CA
Raspberry Pinwheels.....................34 CO	Striped Corners .... 106 CO	Pork And Rice Dish .... 103 CA
Raspberry Punch,	Relish Cheese Ball........................22 AP	Quick Tuna Casserole ....66 CA
Sparkling ....6 BR	Reuben Bake ....38 CA	Rice Veggie Casserole........... 100 CA
Raspberry Sauce ....22 SD	Rhubarb Betty ....71 TR	Salmon Rice Bake ....77 CA
Raspberry Sauce, Poached	Rhubarb Cobbler, Peachy..............10 SD	Shipwreck...............................29 CA
Peaches In ....22 SD	Rhubarb Crisp .... 114 BR	Shrimp Fried Rice ....78 SF
Raspberry Swirl.............................51 SD	Rhubarb Dumpling Dessert,	Shrimp Salad Wraps ....82 AP
Raspberry Trifles, Mango..............56 TR	Berry.......................................16 SD	Souper Supper .... 113 CA
Ratatouille ....98 SC	Rhubarb Muffins, Strawberry ....22 BR	Southern Turkey Casserole......64 CA
Red Potatoes, Dressed..................36 SC	Rhubarb Pie, Strawberry.................8 SD	Southwestern Casserole........ 100 CA
Red Ribbon Delight ....71 SD	Rhubarb Strawberry Sauce ....34 BR	Special Ham Fried Rice ....94 SF
Red Sweet Sauce ....95 AP	Rib Sauce ....42 MC	Speedy Shrimp........................85 SF
Red Wine Marinade......................36 MC	Ribbon Zucchini Frittata...............60 BR	Spicy Beans And................... 102 SC

MOST LOVED COOKBOOKS KEY: Appetizers **AP** • Brunches **BR** • Casseroles **CA** • Cookies **CO** • Festive Baking **FB** • Holiday Favourites **HF**
Main Courses **MC** • Salads & Dressings **SA** • Slow Cooker Creations **SC** • Stir-fries **SF** • Summertime Desserts **SD** • Treats **TR**

R to S

Sukiyaki Rice Bowl ....28 SF
West Indies Beef ....36 CA
Rice Bowl, Sukiyaki ....28 SF
Rice Medley, Wild .... 102 BR
Rice Noodle Salad, Peanut ....90 SA
Rice Pilaf, Barley And ....71 HF
Rice Rolls, Lentil .... 104 SC
Rice Salad .... 102 SA
Rice Salad, Best .... 100 SA
Rice Salad, Crunchy .... 102 SA
Rice Stuffing Casserole, Wild ....57 HF
Rice Stuffing, Wild .... 118 MC
Rice Stuffing, Wild ....57 HF
Rice Veggie Casserole.................. 100 CA
Rich Chicken Stew..........................86 SC
Rich Dark Fruitcake .... 120 HF
Rio Ranchero Layered Salad ....22 SA
Risotto, Herbed Barley ....32 SC
Riviera Chicken Casserole ....52 CA
Roast Chicken.................................84 MC
Roast Supreme, Turkey ....96 SC
Roast Turkey ....52 HF
Roasted Pecans............................ 117 SA
Roasted Pepper Sauce ....72 BR
Roasts
    Apricot Pork Loin Roast ....58 HF
    Comfort Roast ....60 HF
    Garlic-Stuffed Pork....................68 MC
    Herb-Crusted Pork ....66 MC
    Herbed Beef Tenderloin..............8 MC
    Oven Beef...................................12 MC
    Peppercorn ....6 MC
    Pot..46 SC
    Redcurrant And
        Mustard-Glazed Ham ....50 HF
    Roast Turkey ....52 HF
    Slow Cooker Beef ....12 MC
    Spicy Stuffed Beef ....14 MC
    Stuffed Roast With
        Red Wine Sauce ....15 MC

Roll, Chocolate ....84 TR
Roll, Crispy .... 112 TR
Rolled & Cut-Out Cookies
    Bourbon Cookies ....52 CO
    Jam Jams ....42 CO
    Coconut Cookies ....44 CO
    Coffee Fingers ....46 CO
    Cookie Ornaments .... 114 CO
    Jack-O'-Lantern Cookies .... 118 CO
    Lemon Cookies..........................40 CO
    Lollipop Cookies .... 114 CO
    Mocha Diamonds................... 108 CO
    Raisin Sandwich Cookies ...... 118 CO
    Raisin-Filled Cookies ....48 CO
    Sour Cream Nut Rolls...............50 CO
    Sugar Cookies .... 116 CO
    Thick Molasses Cookies ....54 CO
Rolled Chocolate Shortbread..... 102 CO
Rolled Ginger Cookies .... 114 CO
Rolls & Wraps
    Angel..54 SD
    Beef Sprout Rolls ....68 AP
    Beefy Roll-Ups .... 102 AP
    Coffee-Glazed Cinnamon ....16 BR
    Curried Chicken Rolls .... 102 AP
    Dolmades ....62 AP
    Jiffy Mushroom Rolls................98 AP
    Lettuce Wraps ....86 AP
    Mushroom Rolls ....98 AP
    Pot Stickers .... 118 AP
    Savoury Cheese ....14 BR
    Shrimp Salad Wraps ....82 AP
    Spring Rolls ....88 AP
    Tortilla Roll-Ups ....70 AP
    Tri-Colour Angel........................92 SD
Rolls, see Buns & Rolls
Romanoff, Chicken Noodles.........56 CA
Rosemary Chicken, Margo's..........90 MC
Rosemary Dumplings ....30 SC
Roulade Yule Log, Chocolate ......88 HF

Rouladen, Broiled Herbed ....24 MC
Royal Icing .... 116 CO
Rub, Onion Herb..........................14 MC
Rum Balls .... 106 TR
Rum Balls .... 112 HF
Rum Cake......................................24 FB
Rum Diagonals, Coconut ....44 TR
Rum Fluff, Mango ....50 SD
Rum Fruit Salad............................76 SA
Rum Icing......................................44 TR
Rum Sauce ....86 HF
Rummy Eggnog Muffins ....87 FB

S

Sacher Torte Bites ....78 CO
Saffron Pilaf, Sweet.................. 100 BR
Sage And Apricot Stuffing ....76 BR
Salad Wraps, Shrimp....................82 AP
Salads
    Antipasto Pasta Salad ....90 BR
    Caesar-Dressed Salad ....84 BR
    Cucumber Dill Salad.................80 BR
    Cucumber Mousse ....80 BR
    Dill Pasta Salad ....90 BR
    Lime Pear Salad ....46 HF
    Mandarin Poppy Seed
        Salad....................................44 HF
    Orange Poppy Seed
        Coleslaw ....86 BR
    Peaches And Cream ....78 BR
    Potato Salad ....88 BR
    Scallop Attraction ....40 HF
    Spiced Fruit Salad....................13 HF
    Spiced Fruit Salad....................78 BR
    Spinach Grape Salad ....87 BR
    Summer Crunch Salad ....82 BR
    Tomato Mozzarella Salad ....84 BR
    Vanilla Bean Fruit.....................24 SD
Salmon
    Baked ....70 BR
    Broiled......................................54 MC

MOST LOVED COOKBOOKS KEY: Appetizers **AP** • Brunches **BR** • Casseroles **CA** • Cookies **CO** • Festive Baking **FB** • Holiday Favourites **HF**
Main Courses **MC** • Salads & Dressings **SA** • Slow Cooker Creations **SC** • Stir-fries **SF** • Summertime Desserts **SD** • Treats **TR**

most loved cookbooks compilation index — recipes

S

Cornmeal-Crusted .... 56 MC	Chutney .... 96 AP	Creamy Horseradish Sauce ...... 60 HF
Orange And Dill .... 54 MC	Cinnamon Brandy .... 14 TR	Egg And Parsley Sauce .... 66 HF
Salmon 'Chanted Evening .... 52 MC	Cranberry Sauce .... 42 SC	Liquid Gold Sauce .... 35 BR
Salmon Canapés .... 56 AP	Eggnog .... 78 FB	Lobster Newburg .... 70 BR
Salmon Pasta .... 72 CA	Fudge .... 108 SD	Maple Orange Whipped
Salmon Potato Scallop .... 74 CA	Hazelnut .... 92 MC	Cream .... 98 HF
Salmon Rice Bake .... 77 CA	Homemade Cocktail .... 13 AP	Onion Butter .... 82 HF
Salsa	Honey Garlic .... 46 MC	Poultry Gravy .... 54 HF
Fruity .... 36 AP	Honey Mustard .... 78 MC	Raisin Cream Topping .... 38 BR
Mint Papaya .... 25 AP	Horseradish .... 6 MC	Raisin Sauce .... 50 HF
Papaya Coconut .... 20 MC	Jiffy Hollandaise .... 16 MC	Rhubarb Strawberry Sauce ...... 34 BR
Quick .... 48 AP	Kung Pao .... 102 MC	Roasted Pepper Sauce .... 72 BR
Salsa Dressing, Sassy .... 22 SA	Maple .... 72 AP	Rum Sauce .... 86 HF
Salsa-Stuffed Steak .... 28 MC	Marmalade Orange .... 88 MC	Seafood Sauce .... 38 HF
Sandwiches	Meat .... 14 CA	Sesame Walnut .... 118 SA
Barbecue Shredded Pork ...... 108 SC	Melba .... 28 SD	Spiced Whipped Cream .... 10 BR
Chocolate .... 41 FB	Mushroom Chicken Sauce ...... 90 SC	Streusel .... 71 TR
Cookies, Raisin .... 118 CO	Mushroom Cream .... 112 CA	Summer Fruit .... 79 SA
Ice Cream .... 96 SD	Orange Mascarpone .... 32 SD	Vanilla Sauce .... 87 HF
Mango Macadamia .... 94 SD	Orange Sauce .... 106 SC	Walnut Bran .... 10 SD
Santa's Whiskers .... 45 FB	Plum .... 116 MC	Saucy Asian Dinner .... 96 SF
Saskatoon Pie, Fresh .... 8 SD	Pot Roast Gravy .... 46 SC	Saucy Ginger Beef .... 14 SF
Sassy Salsa Dressing .... 22 SA	Raspberry .... 22 SD	Sauerkraut Beef Dinner .... 63 SC
Satay Soup, Carrot .... 16 SC	Red Sweet .... 95 AP	Sausage And Bread Stuffing,
Satay, Polynesian .... 94 AP	Red Wine .... 15 MC	Spicy .... 44 SC
Sauced Crab Ball .... 12 AP	Rib .... 42 MC	Sausage And Potato Stew .... 115 SC
Saucepan Brownies .... 97 TR	Spanish .... 74 AP	Sausage Casserole, Layered ...... 108 CA
Sauces	Spicy Dipping .... 16 AP	Sausage Strata .... 110 CA
Applesauce .... 42 SC	Warm Caramel .... 80 FB	Sausage Stuffing .... 55 HF
Apricot .... 122 AP	Wine .... 50 MC	Sausage Stuffing .... 84 MC
Apricot .... 70 SA	Sauces & Toppings	Sausage Stuffing Casserole .... 55 HF
Bali .... 76 AP	Applesauce .... 59 HF	Sausage, Fruity Beans And .... 40 SC
Barbecue .... 40 MC	Beefy Bun .... 66 SC	Savoury Cheese Rolls .... 14 BR
Black Bean .... 52 SF	Blueberry Topping .... 34 BR	Savoury Crepes .... 26 BR
Bolognese Sauce .... 69 SC	Chocolate Sour Cream .... 22 TR	Scallop Attraction .... 40 HF
Caramel .... 18 SD	Coconut .... 44 CO	Scallop, Ham Veggie .... 112 CA
Caramel .... 66 TR	Coconut .... 58 FB	Scallop, Salmon Potato .... 74 CA
Cheese .... 92 CA	Coconut .... 8 TR	Scalloped Potatoes, Festive .... 70 HF
Chili Dipping .... 82 AP	Coffee Glaze .... 16 BR	Scallops With Bacon .... 63 AP
Chocolate Fudge .... 66 TR	Cranberry Sauce .... 55 HF	Scaloppine, Stuffed Turkey ...... 120 MC

MOST LOVED COOKBOOKS KEY: Appetizers **AP** • Brunches **BR** • Casseroles **CA** • Cookies **CO** • Festive Baking **FB** • Holiday Favourites **HF**
Main Courses **MC** • Salads & Dressings **SA** • Slow Cooker Creations **SC** • Stir-fries **SF** • Summertime Desserts **SD** • Treats **TR**

S

Scones
- Cream Scones .... 93 FB
- Currant Scones .... 90 FB
- Ginger Scones .... 92 FB
- Orange Cranberry Wedges .... 91 FB

Scotch Broth .... 15 SC
Scotch Shortbread .... 75 TR
Scrambled Breakfast .... 52 BR
Scrambled Eggs, Oven .... 52 BR
Sea Bass À La Caesar .... 56 MC
Seafood Curry Dip .... 30 HF
Seafood Delight .... 82 CA
Seafood Enchiladas .... 84 CA
Seafood Fry, Three .... 74 SF
Seafood In Black Bean Sauce .... 84 SF
Seafood Quiche .... 42 BR
Seafood Sauce .... 38 HF
Seafood, see Fish & Seafood
Seasoning, Cajun .... 62 MC
Secret Caesar .... 28 SA
Secret Caesar Dressing .... 28 SA
Sesame Chicken .... 106 MC
Sesame Chicken .... 41 SF
Sesame Kabobs With Spinach ..... 39 MC
Sesame Pork Balls .... 89 AP
Sesame Pork Stir-Fry .... 92 SF
Sesame Snow Peas .... 120 SF
Sesame Soy Dressing .... 112 SA
Sesame Sticks .... 11 AP
Sesame Walnut Topping .... 118 SA
Sex In A Pan .... 58 TR
Shanghai Noodles .... 122 SF
Shaped & Pressed Cookies
- Almond Balls .... 76 CO
- Almond Finger Cookies .... 119 CO
- Black Forest Cookies .... 78 CO
- Buried Cherry Balls .... 76 CO
- Cherry Winks .... 72 CO
- Choco-Cran Biscotti .... 66 CO
- Chocolate Crinkles .... 64 CO

Chocolate Spritz .... 83 CO
Chocolate-Dipped Nutty
    Biscotti .... 67 CO
Coffee Meringues .... 82 CO
Crackerjack Cookies .... 76 CO
Cranberry White Chocolate
    Cookies .... 58 CO
Dirt Cups .... 60 CO
Easy Peanut Butter Cookies .... 58 CO
Egg Nests .... 62 CO
Filbert Fingers .... 71 CO
Gingersnaps .... 62 CO
Lemon Crackles .... 74 CO
Lemon Meringue Kisses .... 84 CO
Nutty Biscotti .... 67 CO
Orange Spritz .... 83 CO
Peanut Blossoms .... 56 CO
Pecan Balls .... 76 CO
Sacher Torte Bites .... 78 CO
Snickerdoodles .... 70 CO
Spritz .... 82 CO
Strawberry Cream Cookies .... 80 CO
Witch's Fingers .... 119 CO
Shepherd's Pie
- Corny .... 116 SC
- Easy .... 25 CA
- Lamb .... 122 CA
- Vegetable .... 98 CA

Sherry Trifle .... 90 HF
Shipwreck .... 29 CA
Short Ribs .... 42 MC
Shortbread .... 32 FB
Shortbread .... 75 TR
Shortbread .... 98 CO
Shortbread
- Butterscotch .... 32 FB
- Checkerboard .... 28 CO
- Cloverleaf .... 28 CO
- Nutty Cherry .... 99 CO
- Rolled Chocolate .... 102 CO

Scotch .... 75 TR
Whipped .... 102 CO
Whipped .... 44 TR
Shortbread Crust .... 51, 62, 100 SD
Shortbread Crust .... 58 FB
Shortbread Crust, Nutty .... 64 SD
Shortbread Pinwheels .... 28 CO
Shortbread Slices, Lemon .... 114 HF
Shortcake, Strawberry .... 14 SD
Shortcake, Strawberry
    Meringue .... 52 TR
Shortcrust Pastry .... 67 FB
Shredded Pork Sandwiches,
    Barbecue .... 108 SC
Shrimp
- Antipasto .... 46 AP
- Black Bean Shrimp Noodles ... 82 SF
- Broccoli Shrimp Stir-Fry .... 66 SF
- Buttered Steak And .... 22 MC
- Chili Lemon .... 64 AP
- Coconut .... 85 AP
- Five-Spice Shrimp .... 70 SF
- Marinated .... 120 AP
- Pad Thai .... 98 SF
- Pot Stickers .... 118 AP
- Seafood in Black Bean Sauce ... 84 SF
- Speedy Shrimp .... 85 SF
- Surprise Spread .... 6 AP
- Sweet-And-Sour Shrimp .... 80 SF
- Three Seafood Fry .... 74 SF

Shrimp And Artichokes .... 68 SF
Shrimp And Asparagus
    Stir-Fry .... 70 SF
Shrimp And Pea Stir-Fry .... 81 SF
Shrimp And Pork Noodles .... 86 SF
Shrimp Ball .... 31 AP
Shrimp Casserole .... 81 CA
Shrimp Chow Mein .... 44 SF
Shrimp Cocktail .... 115 AP
Shrimp Cocktail .... 38 HF

MOST LOVED COOKBOOKS KEY: Appetizers **AP** • Brunches **BR** • Casseroles **CA** • Cookies **CO** • Festive Baking **FB** • Holiday Favourites **HF**
Main Courses **MC** • Salads & Dressings **SA** • Slow Cooker Creations **SC** • Stir-fries **SF** • Summertime Desserts **SD** • Treats **TR**

S

Shrimp Creole ....77 SF
Shrimp Ecstasy ....72 SF
Shrimp Fried Rice ....78 SF
Shrimp Frittata Muffins,
    Pea And ....58 BR
Shrimp Mango Curry ....64 MC
Shrimp Pasta Salad ....86 SA
Shrimp Salad Wraps ....82 AP
Shrimp Salad, Apple And ....44 SA
Shrimp Salad, Japanese ....52 SA
Shrimp Spread ....30 AP
Side Dishes
    Applesauce ....42 SC
    Bacon Varenyky ....82 HF
    Barley And Rice Pilaf ....71 HF
    Bean Sprouts And Peppers ... 120 SF
    Braised Vegetables .... 116 SF
    Broccoli Casserole ....76 HF
    Cabbage Rolls ....80 HF
    Carrot Onion Bake ....38 SC
    Cashew Vegetable Stir-Fry .... 110 SF
    Chicken Fried Rice ....78 SF
    Chicken Vegetable
        Fried Rice ....64 SF
    Chinese Stir-Fry
        Vegetables .... 106 SF
    Cinnamon Honey Carrots ....76 HF
    Confetti Beans ....78 HF
    Corn Pudding ....97 BR
    Cranberry Sauce ....42 SC
    Creamed Spinach ....98 BR
    Dressed Red Potatoes ....36 SC
    Festive Scalloped Potatoes ....70 HF
    Fresh Broccoli Casserole ....76 HF
    Fried Honey Greens .... 116 SF
    Fried Varenyky ....82 HF
    Fruity Beans And Sausage ....40 SC
    Glazed Dill Carrots ....96 BR
    Glazed Parsnips ....68 HF
    Green Bean Stir-Fry .... 106 SF

Herbed Barley Risotto ....32 SC
Instant Glazed Parsnips ....68 HF
Lemon Cranberry Couscous . 102 BR
Lemon Pepper Greens ....96 BR
Lentil Potato Mash ....37 SC
Make-Ahead Potatoes ....36 SC
Marmalade-Glazed Sweet
    Potatoes ....74 HF
Noodle Baskets ....24 SF
Orange-Sauced Beets ....78 HF
Oven Hash Browns ....92 BR
Pan-Fried Noodles ....22 SF
Potatoes Extraordinaire ....68 HF
Sausage Stuffing ....55 HF
Sausage Stuffing Casserole ......55 HF
Sesame Snow Peas .... 120 SF
Shanghai Noodles .... 122 SF
Shrimp Fried Rice ....78 SF
Slow Cooker Dolmades ....34 SC
Special Ham Fried Rice ....94 SF
Spiced Hash Brown
    Potatoes ....92 BR
Spiced Sweet Potato Hash ....94 BR
Spicy Sausage And Bread
    Stuffing ....44 SC
Stuffing ....43 SC
Stuffing Balls ....56 HF
Sufferin' Succotash ....38 SC
Sweet And Smoky
    Brussels Sprouts ....72 HF
Sweet Bean Pot ....40 SC
Sweet Potato Casserole ....75 HF
Sweet Saffron Pilaf .... 100 BR
Turnip Cheese Casserole ....74 HF
Varenyky With Onion
    Butter ....82 HF
Vegetable Couscous .... 118 SF
Vegetable Medley ....98 BR
Veggie Potato Cakes ....94 BR
Wild Rice Medley .... 102 BR

Wild Rice Stuffing ....57 HF
Wild Rice Stuffing Casserole ....57 HF
Yorkshire Pudding ....62 HF
Simple Mayonnaise Dressing ....27 SA
Simple Stuffed Mushrooms ....35 HF
Six Layer Dessert ....58 TR
Skewers
    Beef Kabobs With Oregano
        And Onion ....36 MC
    Bulgogi ....38 MC
    Sesame Kabobs With
        Spinach ....39 MC
Skewers, see Kabobs
Skinny Monkey Bread ....20 BR
Slaw, Broccoli ....48 SA
Slaw, Creamy Celery Seed ....54 SA
Slice, Chocolate Cherry ....94 TR
Slice, Glimmering ....61 TR
Slow Cooker Baked Ham .... 114 SC
Slow Cooker Beef Roast ....12 MC
Slow Cooker Dolmades ....34 SC
Slow Cooker Fajitas ....64 SC
Slow Cooker Lamb Curry .... 118 SC
Slow Cooker Wassail ....20 HF
Slow Stroganoff Stew ....62 SC
Smoked Salmon Muffins ....24 BR
Smoothies, Mango ....8 BR
Smothered Halibut ....78 CA
Snackies, Mexican ....54 AP
Snackin' Potato Skins ....61 AP
Snapper
    Blackened ....62 MC
    Fish And Fennel Parcels ......60 MC
    Fry, Dilled ....76 SF
Snickerdoodles ....70 CO
Snow Peas, Sesame .... 120 SF
Snowballs .... 115 HF
Soft Molasses Drops ....49 TR
Sorbets
    Ginger .... 118 SD

MOST LOVED COOKBOOKS KEY: Appetizers **AP** • Brunches **BR** • Casseroles **CA** • Cookies **CO** • Festive Baking **FB** • Holiday Favourites **HF**
Main Courses **MC** • Salads & Dressings **SA** • Slow Cooker Creations **SC** • Stir-fries **SF** • Summertime Desserts **SD** • Treats **TR**

S

Kiwifruit	120	SD
Mango Melon	120	SD
Soufflé Clouds, Orange	59	SD
Souper Supper	113	CA

Soups
Beef Vegetable Soup	14	SC
Carrot Satay Soup	16	SC
Chicken And Dumpling Soup	30	SC
Chinese Mushroom Soup	12	SC
Chunky Zucchini Soup	20	SC
Cock-A-Leekie	28	SC
Curried Cauliflower Soup	21	SC
French Onion Soup	14	SC
Jazzy Jerk Soup	26	SC
Lobster Chowder	39	HF
Manhattan Clam Chowder	18	SC
Pasta e Fagioli	24	SC
Scotch Broth	15	SC
Split Pea Soup	29	SC
Squash And Lentil Soup	25	SC
Tex-Mex Taco Soup	22	SC
Turkey Mixed Bean Soup	42	HF

Sour Cream
Sour Cream Dressing	20	SA
Sour Cream Nut Rolls	50	CO
Sour Cream Salad, Cucumber	72	SA

Sour Cream Topping,
Caramel Fruit Dip	19	AP
Chocolate	22	TR
Cucumbers In	58	SA
Devil's Dip	12	AP
Dilly Dip	17	AP
Double Devil's Dip	12	AP
Refried Bean Dip	52	AP
Spinach Dip #2	26	AP
Southern Turkey Casserole	64	CA
Southwestern Casserole	100	CA
Soy Dressing	66	SA
Soy Dressing, Sesame	112	SA
Soy Fire Dip	28	AP
Spanish Meatballs	74	AP
Spanish Sauce	74	AP
Sparkling Raspberry Punch	6	BR
Special Caramel Corn	60	AP
Special Ham Fried Rice	94	SF
Special Spiced Coffee	10	BR
Speedy Chicken	110	MC
Speedy Shrimp	85	SF
Spice Coating, Steak With	20	MC
Spiced Coffee, Special	10	BR
Spiced Cranberry Stuffing	122	MC
Spiced Fruit Muffins	88	FB
Spiced Fruit Salad	13	HF
Spiced Fruit Salad	78	BR
Spiced Hash Brown Potatoes	92	BR
Spiced Nuts	118	SA
Spiced Sweet Potato Hash	94	BR
Spiced Whipped Cream	10	BR
Spicy Balsamic Chicken	46	SF
Spicy Beans And Rice	102	SC
Spicy Beef And Broccoli	26	SF
Spicy Dads	11	CO
Spicy Dipping Sauce	16	AP
Spicy Ranch Dressing	64	SA
Spicy Sausage And Bread Stuffing	44	SC
Spicy Stuffed Beef	14	MC

Spinach
Creamed Spinach	98	BR
Eggs Florentine	50	BR
Sesame Kabobs With	39	MC
Spinach And Bacon Omelette	56	BR
Spinach And Cheese Roll	72	BR
Spinach Cheese Pie	46	BR
Spinach Grape Salad	87	BR
Tomato Mozzarella Salad	84	BR
Spinach And Bacon Omelette	56	BR
Spinach And Cheese Roll	72	BR
Spinach And Onions, Cornmeal Flatbread With	92	AP
Spinach Cheese Pie	46	BR
Spinach Dip #1	26	AP
Spinach Dip #2	26	AP
Spinach Grape Salad	87	BR
Spinach Mushroom Salad	26	SA
Spinach Pasta Salad	82	SA
Spinach Squash Salad	38	SA
Split Pea Soup	29	SC
Sponge Custard, Lemon	120	BR
Spreading Forest Fire	38	AP

Spreads
Blue Cheesecake	44	AP
Brie In Pastry	35	AP
Chili Cheese Log	42	AP
Corned Beef Mousse	30	AP
Crab Mousse	32	AP
Cuke Spread 'R Dip	22	AP
Ham And Cheese	34	AP
Ham And Cheese Ball	34	AP
Jalapeño Cheese	24	AP
Jalapeño Jelly	24	AP
Layered Camembert	50	AP
Oriental Cheese	18	AP
Relish Cheese Ball	22	AP
Sauced Crab Ball	12	AP
Shrimp	30	AP
Shrimp Ball	31	AP
Surprise	6	AP
Spring Rolls	88	AP
Spritz	82	CO
Spritz, Chocolate	83	CO
Spritz, Orange	83	CO

Squares, Bars & Brownies
Apricot Zings	89	TR
Bliss Bars	53	FB
Blondie Brownies	60	FB
Butterscotch Confetti	81	TR
Candy Bar Squares	92	TR

MOST LOVED COOKBOOKS KEY: Appetizers **AP** • Brunches **BR** • Casseroles **CA** • Cookies **CO** • Festive Baking **FB** • Holiday Favourites **HF** Main Courses **MC** • Salads & Dressings **SA** • Slow Cooker Creations **SC** • Stir-fries **SF** • Summertime Desserts **SD** • Treats **TR**

S

Caramel Chocolate Squares .....63 FB
Cherry Squares ....88 TR
Chinese Chews ....59 FB
Chocolate Cherry Slice ....94 TR
Chocolate Coconut Melts.......98 TR
Chocolate Crisps ....74 TR
Chocolate Roll ....84 TR
Cream Cheese Brownies........62 FB
Cream Cheese Brownies........96 TR
Double-Chocolate Minis.........60 FB
Fruit And Honey Bars............56 FB
Fudgy Macaroons..................80 TR
Hint O' Mint Squares ....52 FB
Lemon Bars ....84 TR
Lemon Crunch ....90 TR
Lemon Meringue Squares .... 118 BR
Mars Bars Squares ....74 TR
Matrimonial Squares ....86 TR
Midnight Mints ....76 TR
Millionaire Squares ....78 TR
Mincemeat Squares ....56 FB
Nanaimo Bars.......................72 TR
Neapolitan Squares ....54 FB
Orange Date Bars .... 116 BR
Pudding Brownies .... 116 BR
Raspberry Bars ....58 FB
Saucepan Brownies ....97 TR
Scotch Shortbread.................75 TR
Shortbread ....75 TR
Swirl Squares ....80 TR
Take-Along Breakfast
  Bars ....98 TR
Tropical Marshmallow
  Squares......................... 117 BR
Tweed Squares.....................82 TR
Squares, see Bars & Cookies
Squash And Dumplings.........98 SC
Squash And Lentil Soup ....25 SC
Squash Salad, Spinach ....38 SA
Squash Stew.........................32 CA
Steak
  A Round Of Draft ....10 MC
  Acapulco Beef Filet ....25 MC
  Beef And Yam Stew ....34 MC
  Beef Bourguignon ....32 MC
  Beef In Pastry....................18 MC
  Beef Kabobs With Oregano
    And Onion ....36 MC
  Beef Oscar ....16 MC
  Broiled Herbed Rouladen..24 MC
  Bulgogi............................38 MC
  Buttered Steak And Shrimp .....22 MC
  Chinese Pepper ....52 SC
  Honey Ham ....78 MC
  Orange Pork.....................72 MC
  Salsa-Stuffed ....28 MC
  Sesame Kabobs With
    Spinach ....39 MC
  Swiss Stew.......................33 MC
  Tournados ....28 MC
  Veal Oscar ....16 MC
  Zesty Broiled ....24 MC
Steak Bake............................60 SC
Steak Casserole, Swiss ....30 CA
Steak With Mushrooms
  And Onions ....30 MC
Steak With Spice Coating......20 MC
Steamed Fruit Pudding ....84 HF
Stews
  Beef And Yam.................34 MC
  Dijon Beef........................49 SC
  Ginger Beef ....56 SC
  Meatball ....70 SC
  Moroccan Lamb.............. 122 SC
  Oven ....32 CA
  Porcupine Meatball ....20 CA
  Rich Chicken ....86 SC
  Sausage And Potato .... 115 SC
  Slow Stroganoff................62 SC
  Squash.............................32 SC
Swiss....................................33 MC
Sticky Date Pudding.............80 FB
Sticky Ginger Fig Cake ....14 TR
Stilton Puffs ....32 HF
Stir-Fried Honey Greens ..... 116 SF
Stir-Fry
  Kung Pao Chicken.......... 102 MC
  Lemon Grass Pork............76 MC
  Shrimp Mango Curry ....64 MC
Stollen............................... 112 FB
Stollen Tea Dunkers ....50 FB
Strata
  Breakfast..........................40 BR
  Cheese .... 102 CA
  Fiesta...............................39 BR
  Pepper And Ham..............18 HF
  Sausage .... 110 CA
Strawberries In Almond
  Liqueur ....25 SD
Strawberries With Orange
  Custard............................26 SD
Strawberry Banana Frozen
  Yogurt .... 116 SD
Strawberry Cream Cookies....80 CO
Strawberry Cream Layers .....14 SD
Strawberry Dressing ....14 SA
Strawberry Filling ....80 CO
Strawberry Freeze.............. 102 SD
Strawberry Margarita Pie.....78 SD
Strawberry Meringue
  Shortcake ....52 TR
Strawberry Pecan Salad........14 SA
Strawberry Pudding, Croissant.. 114 BR
Strawberry Rhubarb Muffins ....22 BR
Strawberry Rhubarb Pie.........8 SD
Strawberry Sauce, Rhubarb ....34 BR
Strawberry Shortcake ....14 SD
Streusel Muffins, Apple...... 120 TR
Streusel Topping ....71 TR
Striped Corners .... 106 CO

MOST LOVED COOKBOOKS KEY: Appetizers **AP** • Brunches **BR** • Casseroles **CA** • Cookies **CO** • Festive Baking **FB** • Holiday Favourites **HF** • Main Courses **MC** • Salads & Dressings **SA** • Slow Cooker Creations **SC** • Stir-fries **SF** • Summertime Desserts **SD** • Treats **TR**

S

Stroganoff Stew, Slow .... 62 SC
Stroganoff, No-Fuss .... 49 MC
Strudel Dessert, Cherry .... 24 FB
Stuffed Beef, Spicy .... 14 MC
Stuffed Breasts Of Chicken .... 88 MC
Stuffed Chicken Rolls .... 78 SC
Stuffed Meatloaf, Mushroom- ...... 44 MC
Stuffed Mushrooms, Blue .... 35 HF
Stuffed Mushrooms, Simple .... 35 HF
Stuffed Peppers, Corn
   And Bean- .... 92 SC
Stuffed Pork Loin .... 76 BR
Stuffed Pork Roast, Garlic- .... 68 MC
Stuffed Roast With Red
   Wine Sauce .... 68 MC
Stuffed Steak, Salsa- .... 28 MC
Stuffed Tomato Salad .... 84 SA
Stuffed Turkey Breast .... 122 MC
Stuffed Turkey Scaloppine .... 120 MC
Stuffing .... 43 SC
Stuffing
   Apple .... 84 MC
   Bread .... 84 MC
   Chicken 'N' .... 48 SF
   No-Fuss .... 84 MC
   Raisin 'N' Bread .... 14 MC
   Sage And Apricot .... 76 BR
   Sausage .... 84 MC
   Sausage Stuffing .... 55 HF
   Sausage Stuffing Casserole ...... 55 HF
   Spiced Cranberry .... 122 MC
   Spicy Sausage And Bread .... 44 SC
   Stuffing Balls .... 56 HF
   Wild Rice .... 118 MC
   Wild Rice Stuffing .... 57 HF
   Wild Rice Stuffing Casserole ... 57 HF
Stuffing Balls .... 56 HF
Stuffing Meal, Chicken And .... 79 SC
Succotash, Sufferin' .... 38 SC
Sufferin' Succotash .... 38 SC

Sugar Cookies .... 116 CO
Sugar Cookies .... 46 TR
Sugar Cookies, Basic .... 38 FB
Sugar Shapes .... 10 FB
Sugar Syrup, Burnt .... 38 SD
Sugar-Coated Nuts .... 112 AP
Sugary Pizza Crust .... 6 SD
Sukiyaki Rice Bowl .... 28 SF
Summer Crunch Salad .... 82 BR
Summer Fruit Salad .... 78 SA
Summer Fruit Topping .... 79 SA
Sundae Dessert .... 98 SD
Sundaes, Banana Macadamia ...... 66 TR
Sundaes, Peach Melba .... 28 SD
Sun-Dried Tomato Lamb .... 120 SC
Sun-Dried Tomato Turkey Roll ... 68 BR
Surprise Company Dish .... 69 CA
Surprise Spread .... 6 AP
"Sweetish" Meatballs .... 70 SC
Swedish Pastry .... 34 TR
Swedish Tea Cakes .... 34 TR
Sweet And Smoky
   Brussels Sprouts .... 72 HF
Sweet And Sour Wings .... 81 AP
Sweet And Spicy Pork
   Casserole .... 104 CA
Sweet Bean Pot .... 40 SC
Sweet Butter Crust .... 68 FB
Sweet Chili Dressing .... 24 SA
Sweet Creamy Dressing .... 48 SA
Sweet Heat Peanut Chicken .... 92 MC
Sweet Orange Chicken .... 42 SF
Sweet Potato Casserole .... 75 HF
Sweet Potato Dumplings .... 50 CA
Sweet Potato Hash, Spiced .... 94 BR
Sweet Potato Salad .... 94 SA
Sweet Potatoes, Marmalade-
   Glazed .... 74 HF
Sweet Saffron Pilaf .... 100 BR
Sweet Sauce, Red .... 95 AP

Sweet Snacks
   After-Dinner Mints .... 122 TR
   Almond Fruit Bark .... 107 HF
   Apple Loaf .... 118 TR
   Apple Streusel Muffins .... 120 TR
   Apricot Brandy Truffles .... 104 TR
   Breton Brittle .... 106 HF
   Butterscotch Muffins .... 116 TR
   Chipper Muffins .... 116 TR
   Chocolate Brittle .... 100 TR
   Chocolate Cherries .... 110 HF
   Chocolate Marshmallows .... 102 TR
   Chocolate Nuts .... 102 TR
   Choco-Peanut Fudge .... 108 TR
   Cranberry Almond Bark .... 103 TR
   Crispy Roll .... 112 TR
   Five-Minute Fudge .... 108 HF
   Frozen Cheesecake Bites .... 113 TR
   Fudgy Chocolate Mints .... 122 TR
   Lemon Loaf .... 117 TR
   Marshmallow Delights .... 110 TR
   Old-Fashioned Toffee .... 108 HF
   Pinwheels .... 106 TR
   Rum Balls .... 106 TR
   Rum Balls .... 112 HF
   White Chocolate Fudge
      Truffles .... 112 HF
   White Chocolate Popcorn ...... 110 TR
   White Creme Fudge .... 108 TR
Sweet Veggie Dressing .... 40 SA
Sweet Vinaigrette .... 39 SA
Sweet-And-Sour Pork .... 100 SF
Sweet-And-Sour Ribs .... 112 SC
Sweet-And-Sour Shrimp .... 80 SF
Swirl Ice Cream With
   Grilled Cake And Berries .... 48 SD
Swirl Squares .... 80 TR
Swirled Raisin Braid .... 113 FB
Swirling Dervish Cookies .... 40 FB
Swiss Steak Casserole .... 30 CA

MOST LOVED COOKBOOKS KEY: Appetizers **AP** • Brunches **BR** • Casseroles **CA** • Cookies **CO** • Festive Baking **FB** • Holiday Favourites **HF**
Main Courses **MC** • Salads & Dressings **SA** • Slow Cooker Creations **SC** • Stir-fries **SF** • Summertime Desserts **SD** • Treats **TR**

S to T

Swiss Stew .... 33 MC
Swiss Tarts, Baby .... 97 AP
Syrup, Burnt Sugar .... 38 SD
Syrup, Vanilla .... 24 SD
Szechuan Beef .... 36 SF

Tabbouleh .... 94 SA
Table Bread Wreath .... 120 FB
Taco Soup, Tex-Mex .... 22 SC
Take-Along Breakfast Bars .... 98 TR
Take-Along Breakfast Cookies ... 98 TR
Tamale Two-Step, Hot .... 28 CA
Tangy Orange Dressing .... 114 SA
Tarts
   Baby Cheddar .... 97 AP
   Baby Swiss .... 97 AP
   Butter .... 74 FB
   Cheese .... 56 AP
   Crab .... 122 AP
   Cranapple .... 72 FB
   Date And Blue Cheese .... 106 AP
   Jam .... 74 FB
   Mince .... 72 FB
   Mushroom .... 106 AP
Tarts, see Pies & Pastries
Tater-Topped Beef Bake .... 24 CA
Tea Cakes, Swedish .... 34 TR
Tea Ring, Cream Cheese .... 100 FB
Tea Wassail, Hot .... 8 SC
Tea, Fresh Herb .... 9 BR
Teener's Dish .... 11 CA
Tender Beef And Cashews .... 6 SF
Tenderloin, Herbed Beef .... 8 MC
Teriyaki Tofu, Chop-Chop .... 114 SF
Tetrazzini, Chicken .... 54 CA
Tex-Mex Taco Soup .... 22 SC
Thai Noodles .... 18 SF
Thai Pizza On A Garlic Crust ... 104 MC
Thick Molasses Cookies .... 54 CO
Thousand Island Dressing .... 117 SA

Three Pepper Stir-Fry .... 32 SF
Three Seafood Fry .... 74 SF
Thumbprints .... 34 TR
Toast Cups .... 31 AP
Toast Points .... 31 AP
Toast Squares .... 31 AP
Toast Triangles .... 31 AP
Toffee Cookies .... 86 CO
Toffee Slice, Ice Cream .... 96 SD
Toffee, Old-Fashioned .... 108 HF
Tofu And Noodles, Diced .... 112 SF
Tofu, Chop-Chop Teriyaki .... 114 SF
Tomato Basil Pie .... 44 BR
Tomato Mozzarella Salad .... 84 BR
Tomato Pesto Croutons .... 120 SA
Tomato Pineapple Salad .... 62 SA
Tomato Salads
   Chickpea .... 60 SA
   Corn And .... 24 SA
   Stuffed .... 84 SA
Tomato Wine Sauce,
   Lamb Shanks In .... 80 MC
Tomatoes, Freezer .... 64 CA
Toppings, see Sauces & Toppings
Torte, Mango .... 42 SD
Tortilla Bowls .... 32 SA
Tortilla Chips .... 10 AP
Tortilla Crisps .... 10 AP
Tortilla Roll-Ups .... 70 AP
Tortillas
   Beefy Roll-Ups .... 102 AP
   Chips .... 10 AP
   Curried Chicken Rolls .... 102 AP
   Fruity .... 20 SD
   Oven Tortilla Chips .... 10 AP
   Quesadilla Starters .... 111 AP
Tortoni, Macadamia .... 114 SD
Tossed Salad .... 26 SA
Tournados .... 28 MC
Tourtière Québécoise .... 48 MC

Tourtière, French .... 63 HF
Tri-Colour Angel Roll .... 92 SD
Trifles
   Blueberry Lemon .... 122 BR
   Sherry .... 90 HF
   Tropical .... 18 SD
   Truffle .... 54 TR
   Mango Raspberry .... 56 TR
Triple Seafood Noodles .... 67 HF
Tropical Marshmallow
   Squares .... 117 BR
Tropical Trifle .... 18 SD
Truffles
   Apricot Brandy .... 104 TR
   Chocolate .... 22 FB
   White Chocolate Fudge ..... 112 HF
Truffle Trifle .... 54 TR
Tuna Casserole .... 70 CA
Tuna Casserole, Oriental .... 68 CA
Tuna Casserole, Quick .... 66 CA
Tuna
   Antipasto .... 46 AP
Turkey
   Bean And Turkey Bake .... 65 CA
   Creamed Turkey Noodle ...... 62 CA
   Full-Of-Beans Turkey Pot ..... 94 SC
   Pulled Tex Turkey .... 94 SC
   Roast Turkey .... 52 HF
   Southern Turkey Casserole ... 64 CA
   Stuffed Turkey Breast .... 122 MC
   Stuffed Turkey
      Scaloppine .... 120 MC
Turkey À La King .... 47 HF
Turkey Mixed Bean Soup .... 42 HF
Turkey Pies .... 48 HF
Turkey Roast Supreme .... 96 SC
Turkey À La King .... 47 HF
Turkey Mixed Bean Soup .... 42 HF
Turkey Pies .... 48 HF
Turkey Roast Supreme .... 96 SC

MOST LOVED COOKBOOKS KEY: Appetizers **AP** • Brunches **BR** • Casseroles **CA** • Cookies **CO** • Festive Baking **FB** • Holiday Favourites **HF** • Main Courses **MC** • Salads & Dressings **SA** • Slow Cooker Creations **SC** • Stir-fries **SF** • Summertime Desserts **SD** • Treats **TR**

T to W

Turnip Cheese Casserole .... 74 HF
Turnovers, Mushroom .... 66 AP
Turtle Cheesecake .... 10 FB
Tweed Squares .... 82 TR

Upside-Down Lemon Pie .... 56 SD
Uptown Asparagus Chicken .... 66 BR

Vanilla Bean Fruit Salad .... 24 SD
Vanilla Coconut Ice Cream .... 112 SD
Vanilla French Toast, Baked .... 36 BR
Vanilla Icing .... 82, 88 TR
Vanilla Sauce .... 87 HF
Vanilla Syrup .... 24 SD
Vanilla Wafer Crust .... 92 HF
Varenyky With Onion Butter .... 82 HF
Varenyky, Bacon .... 82 HF
Varenyky, Fried .... 82 HF
Veal Cutlets In Wine Sauce .... 50 MC
Veal Oscar .... 16 MC
Vegetable Couscous .... 118 SF
Vegetable Curry .... 100 SC
Vegetable Dip, Best .... 14 AP
Vegetable Fried Rice,
    Chicken .... 64 SF
Vegetable Macaroni,
    Crunchy .... 88 CA
Vegetable Marinade .... 51 SA
Vegetable Medley .... 98 BR
Vegetable Salad, Chunky .... 40 SA
Vegetable Shepherd's Pie .... 98 CA
Vegetable Soup, Beef .... 14 SC
Vegetable Stir-Fry, Cashew .... 110 SF
Vegetables, Braised .... 116 SF
Vegetables, Chinese Stir-Fry ..... 106 SF
Vegetarian Pesto Lasagna .... 92 CA
Veggie Casserole, Rice .... 100 CA
Veggie Crustless Quiche,
    Chicken .... 42 BR
Veggie Dressing, Sweet .... 40 SA
Veggie Potato Cakes .... 94 BR
Veggie Salad, Grilled .... 42 SA
Veggie Scallop, Ham .... 112 CA
Vinaigrette .... 104 SA
Vinaigrettes
    Apple Cider .... 110 SA
    Curry .... 100 SA
    Parsley .... 10 SA
    Sweet .... 39 SA
Vinarterta .... 16 FB

Wafer Crust, Vanilla .... 92 HF
Waffles
    Almond .... 32 BR
    Banana .... 32 BR
    Berry Creamy .... 31 BR
Waldorf, Old-Fashioned .... 74 SA
Walnut Bran Topping .... 10 SD
Walnut Crust .... 66 FB
Walnut Raisin Tart .... 66 FB
Walnut Topping, Sesame .... 118 SA
Warm Bacon Dressing .... 34 SA
Warm Bacon Lettuce Salad .... 34 SA
Warm Caramel Sauce .... 80 FB
Warm Chicken Salad .... 46 SA
Wassail
    Brandy .... 20 HF
    Hot Tea .... 8 SC
    Slow Cooker .... 20 HF
Watermelon, Drunken .... 25 SD
Welsh Cakes .... 50 AP
West Indies Beef .... 36 CA
Wheat Crepes .... 26 BR
Whipped Cream, Maple
    Orange .... 98 HF
Whipped Cream, Spiced .... 10 BR
Whipped Shortbread .... 102 CO
Whipped Shortbread .... 44 TR
White Chip Cookies .... 24 CO
White Chocolate Cookies,
    Cranberry .... 58 CO
White Chocolate Fudge
    Truffles .... 112 HF
White Chocolate Glaze .... 13 FB
White Chocolate Ice Cream ...... 112 SD
White Chocolate Icing .... 16 TR
White Chocolate Orange Chill .... 87 SD
White Chocolate Popcorn .... 110 TR
White Chocolate Pound Cake ..... 16 TR
White Creme Fudge .... 108 TR
Wiener Bites .... 75 AP
Wiener Pasta Bake .... 106 CA
Wieners and Beans .... 106 CA
Wild Rice Medley .... 102 BR
Wild Rice Stuffing .... 118 MC
Wild Rice Stuffing .... 57 HF
Wild Rice Stuffing Casserole .... 57 HF
Wine Marinade, Red .... 36 MC
Wine Sauce .... 50 MC
Wine Sauce, Lamb Shanks
    In Tomato .... 80 MC
Wine Sauce, Red .... 15 MC
Wine Sauce, Veal Cutlets In .... 50 MC
Wine, Beef In Red .... 58 SC
Wine
    Cranberry Mulled .... 10 SC
    Mulled .... 10 SC
    Mulled .... 22 HF
Wings
    Bali .... 76 AP
    Buffalo .... 77 AP
    Crusty Parmesan .... 80 AP
    Glazed .... 108 AP
    Oriental .... 108 AP
    Parmesan Chicken .... 80 AP
    Sweet And Sour .... 81 AP
Witch's Fingers .... 119 CO
Wraps, Peanut Pork .... 90 SF
Wraps, see Rolls & Wraps

MOST LOVED COOKBOOKS KEY: Appetizers **AP** • Brunches **BR** • Casseroles **CA** • Cookies **CO** • Festive Baking **FB** • Holiday Favourites **HF**
Main Courses **MC** • Salads & Dressings **SA** • Slow Cooker Creations **SC** • Stir-fries **SF** • Summertime Desserts **SD** • Treats **TR**

Y

Yakitori .... 110 AP
Yam Stew, Beef And .... 34 MC
Yeast Breads
    Chocolate-Filled Rolls .... 108 FB
    Christmas Bread .... 118 FB
    Christmas Tree Buns .... 122 FB
    Cranberry Pecan Bread .... 114 FB
    Cream Cheese
        Danish Pastries .... 102 FB
    Danish Pastries .... 102 FB
    Easy Overnight Buns .... 106 FB
    Freezer Almond
        Cranberry Buns .... 110 FB
    Gingerbread Pull-Aparts .... 104 FB
    Knotty Cinnamon Buns .... 106 FB
    Panettone .... 116 FB
    Stollen .... 112 FB
    Swirled Raisin Braid .... 113 FB
    Table Bread Wreath .... 120 FB
Yogurt
    Easy Fruit Dip .... 19 AP
    Strawberry Banana Frozen .... 116 SD
    Yogurt And Poppy Seed
        Cheesecake, Orange, ... 74 SD
    Yogurt Fruit Dip .... 34 SD
Yorkshire Pudding .... 62 HF
Yule Log, Chocolate Roulade .... 88 HF

Z

Zesty Beef Casserole .... 6 CA
Zesty Broiled Steak .... 24 MC
Zippy Canapés .... 58 AP
Zucchini Frittata, Ribbon .... 60 BR
Zucchini Soup, Chunky .... 20 SC
Zucchini Treats .... 101 AP
Zucchini Wedges, Creamy .... 48 BR
Zucchini, Beef And .... 8 SF

notes

MOST LOVED COOKBOOKS KEY: Appetizers **AP** • Brunches **BR** • Casseroles **CA** • Cookies **CO** • Festive Baking **FB** • Holiday Favourites **HF**
Main Courses **MC** • Salads & Dressings **SA** • Slow Cooker Creations **SC** • Stir-fries **SF** • Summertime Desserts **SD** • Treats **TR**

tips index

A
Almond paste, availability of ....18 BR
Almonds
   to toast................................28 AP
   to toast................................96 MC
   to toast................. 36, 39, 52, 65 SA
Artichokes, drinking wine with......68 SF
Asian feast, menu suggestions .....82 SF
Asparagus
   canned, substitution for ....72 CA
   trimming ....71 SF
   trimming ....81 CA
   using ends ....71 SF
   using ends ....81 CA
Avocados,
   to choose .... 36, 39, 52, 65 SA

B
Bacon, to store cooked ....20 SA
Baking dishes
   choosing size of.........................6 CA
   choosing volume of....................6 CA
   selecting ....10 CA
Baking pans, removing
   from oven ....66 FB
Baking powder,
   to substitute ....64 CO
Baking, blind ....58 SD
Bananas, using overripe ....20 BR
Barbecuing/Grilling
   salmon ....52 MC
   sea bass ....56 MC
   vegetables ....92 MC
Bean sprouts
   availability of ....65 CA
   storing ....65 CA
Bean threads, using ....34 SF
Beans, to rinse and
   drain canned ....58 SA

Beef
   to slice easily ....94 AP
   using inexpensive cuts of ....30 CA
Birthday party, throwing............ 110 SD
Black bean sauce to differentiate
   between products .... 68, 104 AP
Black bean sauce, types of ....17 SF
Blending hot liquids ....16 FB
Bok choy, substitution for .... 116 SF
Bread cubes, drying ....18 HF
Bread, to cut into cubes...............43 SA
Bread, using day-old ....38 BR
Breadcrumbs, making ....70 BR
Broiling peppers ....42 SA
Broiling vegetables ....42 SA
Brown sugar, to soften............. 110 CO
Butter, baking with cold............ 110 BR
Buttermilk, substitution for............8 HF
Button mushrooms
   purchasing ....30 SF
   washing ....30 SF

C
Cabbage rolls, preventing
   sticking....................................80 HF
Cabbage, choosing ....19 CA
Cake
   angel food, cooling ....40 SD
   angel food, cutting..................39 SD
Cake flour, substitution for...........40 SD
Candy thermometers,
   calibrating ....24 HF
Candy, hard, crushing..................46 FB
Canned beans, to rinse
   and drain.................................58 SA
Cantaloupe, selecting...................12 SD
Capers, rinsing ....24 BR
Caramel, ribbon stage of.............70 FB

Caraway seeds, using...................63 SC
Cardamom, bruising ....88 SC
Cashews, to toast.........................56 SA
Casserole, designing
   your own............................. 114 CA
Casseroles, doneness test for........14 CA
Cauliflower, storing .... 118 SC
Celery
   reviving wilted.........................58 SF
   storing.....................................60 CA
   to store....................................18 SA
Cheese, choosing..........................70 CA
Chicken wings
   to freeze ....76, 77, 80, 81, 108 AP
   to make
      ahead ......76, 77, 80, 81, 108 AP
   to separate whole wings ....76 AP
Chicken, cooked,
   substitution for ....56 CA
Chicken, substituting
   leftover ....42 BR
Chilies, to wash and chop......... 102 MC
Chipotle peppers, storing.......... 102 SC
Chocolate, to melt
   in microwave...........................71 CO
Choosing avocados ....16 SA
Choosing corn on the cob ....24 SA
Chopstick etiquette.....................60 SF
Chopsticks, using ....14 SF
Cilantro and parsley,
   differentiating..........................84 CA
Cilantro, to substitute
   parsley for ....36 AP
Citrus
   juicing and zesting ....23 HF
   zesting and juicing ....12 FB
   zesting and juicing ....56 SD

MOST LOVED COOKBOOKS KEY: Appetizers **AP** • Brunches **BR** • Casseroles **CA** • Cookies **CO** • Festive Baking **FB** • Holiday Favourites **HF**
Main Courses **MC** • Salads & Dressings **SA** • Slow Cooker Creations **SC** • Stir-fries **SF** • Summertime Desserts **SD** • Treats **TR**

C to J

Citrus fruit
  segmenting .... 8 BR
  zesting and juicing .... 120 BR
Citrus stripper,
  to create "stripes" .... 14 AP
Coconut
  to toast .... 106 CO
  to toast .... 20 MC
  to toast .... 76, 103 SA
  toasting .... 108 BR
  toasting .... 16, 88 SC
  toasting .... 48 SD
  toasting .... 72 HF
  toasting .... 96 FB
Coffee
  making .... 16 BR
  storing .... 16 BR
Cookies, cooling .... 109 HF
Cooling cookies .... 46 CO
Corn on the cob,
  to choose .... 24 SA
Corned beef to substitute
  for canned .... 30 AP
Cornstarch, using .... 42 SF
Crinkle cutter, to make
  ruffled edges .... 14 AP
Crushed cookies,
  to prevent .... 32 CO
Cutting bread into cubes .... 43 SA

Daikon
  choosing .... 12 SF
  storing .... 12 SF
Dessert buffet,
  hosting .... 66 FB
Drop cookies, to make
  uniformly sized .... 6 CO
Drumettes, see Chicken wings
Dry measures, using .... 17 BR
Drying lettuce leaves .... 38 SA

Egg yolks, uses for .... 38 SD
Eggnog, substitution for .... 87, 94 FB
Eggs
  making hard-cooked .... 88 BR
  raw, using .... 22, 24, 116 HF
  raw, using .... 83 SD
  to make perfect
    hard-boiled .... 59 AP
  to slice hard-boiled easily .... 59 AP
Electric griddle,
  substituting .... 28 BR

Fat to reduce in salads .... 104 SA
Filling a piping bag .... 84 CO
Flattened dough logs,
  to prevent .... 96 CO
Food colouring,
  paste versus liquid .... 38 FB
Freezer pop forms,
  substitution for .... 109 SD
Freezing
  chicken
    wings .... 76, 77, 80, 81, 108 AP
  cookies .... 19, 56 CO
  meatballs .... 46 MC
  meatballs ..... 72, 74, 96, 100, 122 AP
  tarts .... 56, 97, 106, 107, 122 AP
  tomato paste .... 34 MC
Frozen desserts, cutting .... 95 SD
Fruit tray, preparing .... 78 BR
Fruit, fresh, cooking with .... 23 SD
Fruitcakes, baking .... 8 FB
Fruitcakes, storing .... 8 FB
Fruits and vegetables,
  servings .... 10 SF
Frying pan, covering
  handle with foil .... 59 BR

Garlic
  exposure to air .... 52 SF

  to store .... 64 SA
Ginger
  fresh and dried .... 16 SF
  storing .... 16 SF
Glaze, making .... 122 FB
Grating lemon zest .... 40 CO
Gravy
  reducing greasiness of .... 54 HF
  reducing lumps .... 54 HF
  substitutions for .... 48 CA
Greek feast, menu
  suggestions .... 120 CA
Gumdrops, cutting .... 118 HF

Ham
  ready-to-serve .... 78 MC
  baked, basting .... 75 BR
Handling hot peppers
  and chilies .... 22 SA
Hands, to keep odour-free .... 122 SA
Hard cookies, to soften .... 25 CO
Hard-boiled eggs
  to make perfect .... 59 AP
  to slice easily .... 59 AP
Hard-cooked egg, making
  the perfect .... 10 SA
Hazelnuts to toast .... 92 MC
Herbs
  growing .... 76 SF
  storing dried .... 58 CA
Horseradish
  fresh, using .... 114 SC
  storing .... 76 CA
Hot peppers and chilies,
  to handle .... 22 SA
Hot peppers to
  chop safely .... 36, 48 AP

Imitation crab, uses for .... 82 CA

MOST LOVED COOKBOOKS KEY: Appetizers **AP** • Brunches **BR** • Casseroles **CA** • Cookies **CO** • Festive Baking **FB** • Holiday Favourites **HF**
Main Courses **MC** • Salads & Dressings **SA** • Slow Cooker Creations **SC** • Stir-fries **SF** • Summertime Desserts **SD** • Treats **TR**

J to P

J
Jellied salads, molding .... 46 HF
Jelly salad, to unmold .... 68 SA
Julienne vegetables, cutting ...... 110 SF
Julienne, cutting .... 71 HF
Julienning .... 60 BR

K
Kitchen shears,
  kids cutting with .... 26 SF
Kiwifruit
  selecting .... 6 SD
  storing .... 6 SD

L
Leeks, cleaning .... 41 SF
Lemon zest, to grate .... 40 CO
Lemon, to zest and juice .... 74 CO
Lemons, zesting
  before juicing .... 104 SC
Lettuce
  to dry leaves .... 38 SA
  to remove core .... 6 SA
Lime cordial, uses for .... 18 SD
Loaves, storing .... 94 FB

M
Making the perfect
  hard-cooked egg .... 10 SA
Mangoes to choose
  ripe fruit .... 64 MC
Maraschino cherry juice
  substitution for .... 54 FB
Marinades to add flavour .... 66 MC
Marinated salads,
  easy preparation .... 61 SA
Marshmallow garnishes,
  making .... 112 BR
Meat
  browning .... 122 SC
  browning .... 34 CA
  inexpensive cuts of .... 60 SC
  portion sizes .... 58 HF
  slicing .... 20 SF
  slicing .... 56 SC

Meat mallet, substituting .... 68 BR
Meatballs
  to freeze .... 46 MC
  to freeze ..... 72, 74, 96, 100, 122 AP
  to make
    ahead .... 72, 74, 96, 100, 122 AP
  to make uniform size .... 72 AP
Melting chocolate
  in the microwave .... 71 CO
Melting wafers, purchasing .... 15 SD
Meringue, making .... 118 BR
Mexican fiesta
  menu suggestions .... 28 CA
  menu suggestions .... 50 SF
Milk, soured, making .... 30, 48 SC
Mincemeat, smoother
  texture .... 72 FB
Mushrooms
  to substitute canned .... 66 AP
  cleaning .... 72 SC
Mustard, dry, substitution for .... 102 CA

N
Noodles, reducing
  stickiness of .... 112 SF
Nuts
  to make ahead .... 112 AP
  to toast .... 26, 106 CO
  to toast .... 28 AP
  toasting .... 108 BR
  toasting .... 16, 88 SC
  toasting .... 48 SD
  toasting .... 56 SF
  toasting .... 72 HF
  toasting .... 93 CA
  toasting .... 96 FB

O
Olive oil, to store .... 108 SA
Omelette toppings,
  experimenting with .... 54 BR
Onion soup, substitution for .... 12 CA

Onion, to keep hands
  odour-free .... 122 SA
Onions, chopping .... 39 BR
Oranges, segmenting .... 36 SA
Oven temperature .... 60 CO
Over-browning, to prevent .... 22 CO
Overcooking food .... 21 SC
Over-handling dough,
  to prevent .... 42 CO

P
Pad Thai, serving .... 98 SF
Pancetta, storing .... 69 SC
Paprika, storing .... 112 CA
Parsley as substitute
  for cilantro .... 36 AP
Parsnips, choosing .... 78 CA
Passion fruit, ripening .... 42 SD
Pasta
  cooking .... 88 SF
  cooking .... 91 BR
  reducing stickiness of .... 62 CA
Pearl onions, peeling .... 32, 98 MC
Pecans
  storing .... 102 SD
  to toast .... 62 SA
Peeling pearl onions .... 32, 98 MC
Peppers, bell
  choosing .... 77 SF
  storing .... 77 SF
Peppers, hot
  handling .... 44, 64, 91, 102, 105 SC
  handling .... 62 SF
  reducing heat of .... 91, 105 SC
  to chop safely .... 36, 48 AP
Peppers, roasting .... 72 BR
Peppers, to broil .... 42 SA
Pie shells, baking .... 60 SD
Pimientos, uses for .... 26 CA
Pine nuts, to toast .... 82, 87 SA
Piping bag, to fill .... 84 CO

MOST LOVED COOKBOOKS KEY: Appetizers **AP** • Brunches **BR** • Casseroles **CA** • Cookies **CO** • Festive Baking **FB** • Holiday Favourites **HF**
Main Courses **MC** • Salads & Dressings **SA** • Slow Cooker Creations **SC** • Stir-fries **SF** • Summertime Desserts **SD** • Treats **TR**

most loved cookbooks compilation index

tips | 43

P to T

Porcelain, cleaning ....82 SD
Pork, freezing .... 103 CA
Potato, substituting leftover ....64 BR
Pots, aluminum, cleaning..............82 SD
Preparing marinated salads ....61 SA
Preventing cookies crushing..........32 CO
Preventing over-browning............22 CO
Preventing over-handling.............42 CO
Pudding containers, buying ....84 HF
Pumpkin, canned, storing ....97 FB
Punch, chilling ....20 HF

R

Raw meat safety ....79 SC
Ready-to-serve ham....................78 MC
Reducing fat in salads............... 104 SA
Removing core from lettuce...........6 SA
Rice noodles, cooking ....96 SF
Rice
  brown and white,
    interchanging....................42 CA
  cold cooked, using ....64 SF
  fried, adding egg to ....78 SF
  varieties of .... 100 SF
Ripe mangoes to choose.............64 MC
Round cookie dough logs ....96 CO
Rubs to add flavour ....66 MC
Rum, spiced
  substitution for ....50 FB

S

Saffron, purchasing ....40 CA
Saffron, substitution for...............40 CA
Salad greens, drying....................87 BR
Salmon
  canned, choosing....................72 CA
  to barbecue ....52 MC
Sauce, black bean to differentiate
  between products .... 68, 104 AP
Sauces to thicken ....90 MC
Scallops
  choosing ....84 SF

cooking ....40 HF
cooking ....84 SF
Scones, soft-sided, making...........93 FB
Sea bass to grill frozen ....56 MC
Seafood
  freezing ....74 SF
  storing ....74 SF
  thawing ....74 SF
Seeds
  toasting .... 108 BR
  toasting .... 16, 88 SC
  toasting ....48 SD
  toasting ....72 HF
  toasting ....96 FB
Segmenting oranges ....36 SA
Sesame seeds
  storing ....93 SF
  to toast .... 18, 28, 68, 104 AP
  to toast .... 24, 38, 104, 106 MC
  to toast .... 52, 90, 112, 121 SA
Sherry, cooking,
  substitutions for......................54 CA
Shortbread, to make whiter ....98 CO
Shrimp
  to substitute for canned ..... 6, 30 AP
  to thaw ....64 MC
  deveining ....70 SF
Slicing
  Slicing hard-boiled eggs............59 AP
  Slicing, beef ....94 AP
Slow cooker
  cleaning..................................96 SC
  cooking in .... 100 SC
  leftovers................................ 116 SC
  lifting lid of ....92 SC
  recipes, garnishing ....68 SC
  recipes, stirring.......................92 SC
  safety......................................58 SC
  sizes of....................................8 SC
  to use ....12 MC

Snow peas, trimming...................52 SC
Softening brown sugar............. 110 CO
Softening hard cookies................25 CO
Songkran festival,
  menu suggestions ....18 SF
Soufflés, baking..........................59 SD
Sour cream, substitution for........39 CA
Soured milk
  making ....21 BR
  making ....92 FB
Steak
  preserve juices ....28 MC
  to slice...................................38 MC
Stews, storing.............................32 CA
Storing
  celery.....................................18 SA
  cooked bacon strips ....20 SA
  cookies .... 19, 56 CO
  garlic ....64 SA
  olive oil............................... 108 SA
  tomatoes ....62 SA
Strawberries, purchasing.............22 BR
Substitution for
  baking powder.......................64 CO
Suet
  cooking with ....94 HF
  substitution for ....94 HF
Sugar
  brown, softening....................41 SC
  sanding, about ....84 FB
Sugar shapes, making ....10 FB

T

Tapioca, cooking with..................76 FB
Tarts
  to freeze .... 56, 97, 106, 107, 122 AP
  to make
    ahead ... 56, 97, 106, 107, 122 AP
Tea
  making ....9 BR
  storing ....9 BR

MOST LOVED COOKBOOKS KEY: Appetizers **AP** • Brunches **BR** • Casseroles **CA** • Cookies **CO** • Festive Baking **FB** • Holiday Favourites **HF** • Main Courses **MC** • Salads & Dressings **SA** • Slow Cooker Creations **SC** • Stir-fries **SF** • Summertime Desserts **SD** • Treats **TR**

T to Z

Thawing frozen shrimp ....64 MC
Thickening sauces ....90 MC
Toasting
    almonds .... 36, 39, 52, 65 SA
    cashews.......................... 56, 96 SA
    coconut...................... 76, 103 SA
    pecans................................62 SA
    pine nuts .... 82, 87 SA
    sesame seeds....52, 90, 112, 121 SA
Toasting coconut, nuts and seeds ....
.... 20, 24, 38, 92, 96, 104, 106 MC
Toasting nuts and seeds.......................
.... 18, 28, 68, 104 AP
Tomato paste
    freezing .... 24, 62, 91 SC
    storing.......................... 121, 122 CA
    to freeze ....34 MC
Tomatoes
    peeling ....32 SC
    to store..................................62 SA
Tortillas
    varieties of ....90 SF
    warming.....................................20 SD

Truffles, shaping........................ 113 HF
Tuna, canned, choosing...............66 CA
Turkey
    frozen, thawing ....52 HF
    roasting times..........................52 HF
    safety tips ....52 HF
    substituting with ....67 BR

Unmolding a jelly salad................68 SA

Vanilla
    availability of clear .... 106 BR
    clear, purchasing .... 112 HF
Vanilla wafers, purchasing............73 SD
Vegetables
    cooking times of................... 104 SF
    cutting................. 108 SF
    frozen, defrosting ....48 SF
    prepping ahead......................54 SF
    stir-fry, choosing....................38 SF

    to broil ....42 SA
    to grill......................................92 MC
Vinegar, to substitute
    red for white ....30 SA

Waffle iron, using ....32 BR
Washing and chopping
    chilies .... 102 MC
Water chestnuts, improving
    flavour of..................................16 CA
Wet measures, using ....17 BR
Whiter shortbread ....98 CO
Wings, see Chicken wings
Woks
    choosing ....6 SF
    frying pans and ....6 SF
    seasoning ....8 SF

Zesting and juicing a lemon.........74 CO
Zucchini, storing ....82 SC

MOST LOVED COOKBOOKS KEY: Appetizers **AP** • Brunches **BR** • Casseroles **CA** • Cookies **CO** • Festive Baking **FB** • Holiday Favourites **HF**
Main Courses **MC** • Salads & Dressings **SA** • Slow Cooker Creations **SC** • Stir-fries **SF** • Summertime Desserts **SD** • Treats **TR**

additional tips

MOST LOVED COOKBOOKS KEY: Appetizers **AP** • Brunches **BR** • Casseroles **CA** • Cookies **CO** • Festive Baking **FB** • Holiday Favourites **HF**
Main Courses **MC** • Salads & Dressings **SA** • Slow Cooker Creations **SC** • Stir-fries **SF** • Summertime Desserts **SD** • Treats **TR**

additional tips

MOST LOVED COOKBOOKS KEY: Appetizers **AP** • Brunches **BR** • Casseroles **CA** • Cookies **CO** • Festive Baking **FB** • Holiday Favourites **HF** Main Courses **MC** • Salads & Dressings **SA** • Slow Cooker Creations **SC** • Stir-fries **SF** • Summertime Desserts **SD** • Treats **TR**

additional tips

MOST LOVED COOKBOOKS KEY: Appetizers **AP** • Brunches **BR** • Casseroles **CA** • Cookies **CO** • Festive Baking **FB** • Holiday Favourites **HF** • Main Courses **MC** • Salads & Dressings **SA** • Slow Cooker Creations **SC** • Stir-fries **SF** • Summertime Desserts **SD** • Treats **TR**

Copyright © 2009
DRG
306 East Parr Road
Berne, IN 46711

All rights reserved. This publication may not be reproduced in part or in whole without written permission from the publisher.

Every effort has been made to ensure the accuracy and completeness of this index.

Printed in United States of America

ISBN: 978-1-59635-294-0

DRGbooks.com

1 2 3 4 5 6 7 8 9